# Navigating Acad

This engaging collection of recent
career involves not only pursuit of a scholarly discipline but also such
unwelcome features as the tribulations of graduate school, the trials of
teaching, and the tensions that develop from membership in a department. The author, who enjoyed a distinguished career as a professor of
philosophy and senior university administrator, draws on his extensive
experience to offer candid advice about handling the frustrations of
academic life. Combining philosophical principles, practical concerns,
and personal observations, this book serves as a reliable guide for both
new and veteran academics as well as for anyone seeking to understand
the inner workings of colleges and universities.

**Steven M. Cahn** is Professor Emeritus of Philosophy at the City
University of New York Graduate Center, where he served for nearly
a decade as Provost and Vice President for Academic Affairs, then as
Acting President.

# Navigating Academic Life

## How the System Works

Steven M. Cahn

Routledge
Taylor & Francis Group
NEW YORK AND LONDON

First published 2021
by Routledge
52 Vanderbilt Avenue, New York, NY 10017

and by Routledge
2 Park Square, Milton Park, Abingdon, Oxon, OX14 4RN

*Routledge is an imprint of the Taylor & Francis Group, an informa business*

*Library of Congress Cataloging-in-Publication Data*

Names: Cahn, Steven M., author.
Title: Navigating academic life : how the system works / Steven M. Cahn.
Description: New York, NY : Routledge, 2021. | Includes bibliographical references and index.
Identifiers: LCCN 2020027977 (print) | LCCN 2020027978 (ebook) | ISBN 9780367626624 (hardback) | ISBN 9780367626617 (paperback) | ISBN 9781003110163 (ebook)
Subjects: LCSH: Cahn, Steven M. | College teaching--Vocational guidance--United States--Anecdotes. | College teachers--United States--Anecdotes. | Universities and colleges--Administration--Anecdotes. | Universities and colleges--United States--Anecdotes. | College teachers--United States--Biography.
Classification: LCC LB1778.2 .C35 2021 (print) | LCC LB1778.2 (ebook) | DDC 378.0071--dc23
LC record available at https://lccn.loc.gov/2020027977
LC ebook record available at https://lccn.loc.gov/2020027978

ISBN: 978-0-367-62662-4 (hbk)
ISBN: 978-0-367-62661-7 (pbk)
ISBN: 978-1-003-11016-3 (ebk)

Typeset in Stempel Garamond
by SPi Global, India

*To my wife,*
*Marilyn Ross, M.D.*

# Contents

# Acknowledgments

I am grateful to my editor Matthew Friberg for his advice and support and to the staff at Routledge for assistance throughout production. My brother, Victor L. Cahn, playwright and Professor Emeritus of English at Skidmore College, offered innumerable stylistic and substantive suggestions. My wife, Marilyn Ross, M.D., has helped in more ways than I can express in words.

# Preface

Those attracted to a professorial career are typically motivated by enthusiasm for a scholarly discipline. They seek to study a subject in depth, then share their thoughts with those equally devoted to such exploration.

Certain unavoidable aspects of academia, however, may be an unwelcome surprise. First come the tribulations of graduate school, second the trials of teaching, and third the tensions that develop from membership in a department. These facets of academic life are rarely given extended treatment, but here they are my focus.

Several years ago, I was encouraged to submit materials to the blog of the APA (American Philosophical Association) and, finding the format to my liking, sent in numerous posts that, judging by the number of positive responses, were well received. In this book I have reworked these materials into a unified presentation that also draws on the following prior works:

> Cahn, Steven M., *The Eclipse of Excellence: A Critique of American Higher Education*, Public Affairs Press, 1973. Reprinted by Wipf and Stock Publishers, 2004.

_____, *Education and the Democratic Ideal.* Nelson-Hall Company, 1979. Reprinted by Wipf and Stock Publishers, 2004.

_____, *Saints and Scamps: Ethics in Academia.* Rowman and Littlefield, 1986. Revised Edition, 1994. 25th Anniversary Edition, 2011.

_____, *Puzzles & Perplexities: Collected Essays.* Rowman and Littlefield, 2002. Second Edition, 2007.

_____, *From Student to Scholar: A Candid Guide to Becoming a Professor.* Columbia University Press, 2008.

_____, *Teaching Philosophy: A Guide.* Routledge, 2018.

_____, *Inside Academia: Professors, Politics, and Policies.* Rutgers University Press, 2019.

_____, *The Road Traveled and Other Essays.* Wipf and Stock Publishers, 2019.

# Part I
# Graduate School

# Chapter 1

## *Orientation*

Most graduate departments offer entering students an orientation session, but if my former department's approach is typical, the meeting is too often a lost opportunity.

Here is the scene I witnessed every September for many years. Most newcomers arrived unsure or even apprehensive, but all were eager to understand more fully the situation they faced. Few faculty participated in the session, however, and those who did treated the occasion lightly, engaging in banter with one another and evincing little concern for the anxieties of the beginners.

The chair started by inviting the newcomers to introduce themselves and indicate their specialty. Those who replied with uncertainty received patronizing smiles, while the response that invariably caused derisive laughter was, "I plan to teach".

Subsequently the faculty were asked to describe their current scholarly work. The audience listened attentively, nodding as if comprehending every word while struggling to understand any of what was said.

Next, the students were invited to ask about the program but, being unfamiliar with it, did not have much to contribute. The message they received, though, was clear and emphatic: Find an area of research and publish as much as possible. Although nearly all the doctoral students were eventually expected to teach undergraduates, not a word was said about this responsibility. Nor was any advice given about how best to survive the hoops and hurdles of doctoral study. Instead, the session concluded early, when the chair announced that the essentials had been covered and the time had come for wine and cheese.

Perhaps this approach to orientation is unique to my program, but I presume other departments engage in similar practices. I would suggest, however, that we can do better. Here is advice that should prove useful to those heading into academia:

1.  Read widely. As a college student you were responsible only for works the instructor assigned, but as a scholar you create your own reading lists. The more literature you master, the less reliant you are on faculty.
2.  Write frequently. Putting one's ideas into written form aids precise thinking. If you doubt the effectiveness of your style, consult an appropriate handbook.[1]
3.  Don't delay. Do not allow lack of confidence to lead you to put off fulfilling requirements, taking examinations, or submitting papers. The longer you wait, the more the pressure mounts. Postponement is not progress.

4. Meet the professors. Eventually you will need to choose an advisor to guide your dissertation. Whether by attending a lecture, conversing at a departmental function, or visiting during office hours, seek a professor whose interests and personality are in sync with your own.

5. Meet other students. They can offer helpful advice about professors and strategies. Furthermore, discussion with colleagues is one of the pleasures of the profession. Granted, solitude may stimulate creativity, but scholars do not flourish in isolation. Rather, they rely on publishers, librarians, and one another.

6. Meet professional colleagues. Those at other institutions who share your interests can offer valuable contacts. You can encounter such individuals at scholarly conferences, whether you merely attend or, better yet, serve as a speaker, commentator, or session chair. By the way, volunteers are often sought for these positions. Furthermore, because almost all the attendees will be active scholars in your field, they will be as eager to meet you as you are to meet them.

7. Seek a dissertation topic. As you proceed, be alert for a potential project that engages your interest, is of appropriate scope, and is original without being eccentric. Choosing your subject wisely is a crucial step toward finishing your work in a reasonable time and maximizing your chances for a desirable academic position. Publishing along the way is a

plus, but finding a winning dissertation topic is invaluable.

8. Diversify your interests. Don't be a one-trick pony, a scholar with only one area of expertise who offers endless variations on the same theme. At an interview, you may well be asked about your interests apart from your dissertation. You should have a couple you can discuss.

9. Plan to teach. Before long you will be expected to assume the obligations and challenges of teaching undergraduates. Not all your students will have an immediate attraction to your subject. Thus as you proceed, consider how you might motivate students to explore central issues in your discipline.

10. Maintain your dignity. Unfortunately, graduate professors occasionally take advantage of students in various ways, including destructive criticism, inordinate delays in returning work, inaccessibility, or failure to separate professional and personal concerns. Even worse, professors have been involved in countless scandals involving sexual harassment or abuse. In all these instances, students should not abide mistreatment but should immediately report any incidents to the appropriate administrator, whether the department chair or a dean. Thereafter inaction from the authorities should be met with forceful protest.

An orientation meeting that explained these points might take a couple of hours but would be worth attending, even in the absence of refreshments. Furthermore, the session would emphasize to all that the primary aim of doctoral education is not to enhance faculty interests or prerogatives but to support students in their efforts to succeed as scholars and teachers.

## Note

1  See, for example, Steven M. Cahn and Victor L. Cahn, *Polishing Your Prose: How to Turn First Drafts into Finished Work* (New York: Columbia University Press, 2013).

# Chapter 2

## *Choosing a Dissertation Topic*

Much has been written about the challenges of completing a dissertation and avoiding the status of an "ABD", that ironic acronym that refers to someone who has finished **A**ll the requirements for a doctoral degree **B**ut the **D**issertation.[1] My concern here, however, is with an often overlooked aspect of choosing a dissertation subject: In the search for an initial faculty position, the thesis will be regarded as the essence of an individual's academic identity. Thus the topic needs to suit both earning a diploma and finding a position. Yet ironically, a topic that helps to reach the first objective may in fact hinder success in achieving the second. (The following examples come from my own discipline of philosophy, but the concerns presented apply to all other fields in the humanities and social sciences and perhaps to other areas as well.)

Consider a hypothetical student, Pat, who seeks a position in political philosophy but, having become interested in John Dewey's aesthetics, decides to write a dissertation on that subject. The faculty in Pat's department approves the thesis with enthusiasm, yet when Pat is considered for a post in political philosophy, the appointing department not surprisingly prefers a candidate whose dissertation is in political theory, not the theory of art.

Next, consider a student, Chris, who specializes in ethics and decides to write on the moral theory of the nowadays relatively neglected metaphysician Nicolai Hartmann (1882–1950), who viewed values as unchanging ideal entities. This subject may work as a dissertation because few faculty members are likely to be familiar with the details of Hartmann's position and may see the area as worth exploring. But when Chris seeks positions in ethics, most other applicants will have written dissertations devoted to subjects far more likely to be seen as useful in teaching standard undergraduate ethics courses.

A third student, Sandy, wishes to be distinctive by choosing a topic that is outré, such as supporting the morality of severe corporal punishment in order to reduce crime. Perhaps a couple of faculty members in Sandy's department judge the topic as bold, though odd, and pass the thesis. At interviews, however, when asked to explain the work, Sandy faces a skeptical audience, uncomfortable appointing a faculty member who holds such a strange view. In short, most interviewers seek candidates with topics that are innovative, not idiosyncratic.

A fourth student, Leslie, has two major research interests: the history of modern philosophy from Descartes to Kant and the history of Russian philosophy. The former subject is taught in virtually every department, whereas the latter is offered in hardly any; hence many positions call for a specialization in modern philosophy, while virtually none seeks expertise in Russian philosophy. Thus even if Leslie's doctoral faculty includes a specialist in Russian philosophy who encourages students to make that area the focus of their dissertations, Leslie would be well advised to resist such urgings and choose a topic in the history of modern philosophy.

Notice, though, that such decisions require awareness of which specializations are most in demand, information that can be found in available job listings. Admittedly, the number of openings in any particular area will vary from year to year, but departments need to provide coverage for the courses they offer, and curricula rarely change dramatically. That obvious consideration may be overlooked as graduate students follow the lead of professors who have research agendas of their own. The impracticality of their suggestions, however, may become painfully apparent when candidates are called on to explain how their work might be useful in teaching courses regularly offered to undergraduates.

A search for a position is arduous enough without identifying yourself with a dissertation topic that either misrepresents your major focus or does not align with customary materials offered by most departments. Granted, graduate students are entitled to pursue an independent path of inquiry that defies common expectation. Nevertheless, in doing so they are likely to face a special challenge in obtaining an appointment, and they should be alerted to this situation by responsible members of their faculty.

## Note

1  See, for example, Steven M. Cahn, *From Student to Scholar: A Candid Guide to Becoming a Professor* (New York: Columbia University Press, 2008), 7–15.

# Chapter 3

## *The Hidden Curriculum*

Throughout the years of doctoral study, more is learned than the subtleties of research. Messages are passed on subliminally in the "hidden curriculum", the unstated attitudes that are communicated to students as a by-product of school life. Although the phrase is usually employed in the context of elementary or secondary education, the words also apply to the graduate level, where future professors are acculturated to careers in academia.

One implicit message is that prestige follows from accomplishment as a researcher, not as a teacher. For instance, which candidate for a faculty position is usually viewed as more attractive, the promising researcher or the promising teacher? Which of the two is more highly regarded by faculty colleagues? The answers and the lesson are obvious: Excellence in research is judged to be far more important than excellence in teaching.

A second message is that faculty members are entitled to put their own interests ahead of their students. Consider how departments decide graduate course offerings. The procedure is for individual professors to announce the topics of their choice; that conglomeration then becomes the curriculum. The list may be unbalanced or of little use to those preparing for their careers, but such concerns are apt to be viewed as irrelevant. The focus is not on meeting student needs but on satisfying faculty desires.

Similarly, in a course ostensibly devoted to a survey of a major field of philosophy, the instructor may decide to distribute chapters of the instructor's own forthcoming book and ask students to help edit the manuscript. Whether this procedure is the best way to promote understanding of the fundamentals of the announced field is not even an issue.

Another instance of professorial primacy is readers who take months to return a chapter of a dissertation, explaining the delay by pointing to publishing deadlines they themselves face. Apparently the student's deadlines for finishing the dissertation and obtaining a faculty position are not as important.

A third message is that when you listen to a speaker, you should pretend you understand what is being said, even when you don't. How many times do faculty members and students sit through a presentation grasping little or nothing of it, yet unwilling to say so? Instead, they nod as if comprehending every word. In short, contra Socrates, the goal is always to appear knowledgeable.

Yet just the opposite ought to be the case. Professors should encourage students in class to indicate whenever they become confused. And such admissions should be met not with a put-down but with a compliment for intellectual honesty. After all, those afraid to admit what they do not grasp are defenseless against others who indulge in obfuscation.

These days signs around the country tell us that if we see something, we should say something. Graduate students should be advised to follow an analogous rule: If you don't understand something, say something.

Professors should be aware of the unstated messages sent to graduate students, who learn from the hidden curriculum and eventually pass it on. Thus are unfortunate attitudes and practices transferred from one generation to another.

# Chapter 4

## *Preparing Graduate Students to Teach*

The hidden curriculum denigrates the importance of teaching, yet an antidote is easy to suggest. The difficulty, however, is finding faculty who care enough to provide it.

The crucial step is requiring that all graduate students seeking a faculty position participate in a departmental colloquium that prepares them for offering effective instruction to undergraduates. For many years I offered such a credit-bearing course in the Philosophy Program at the City University of New York Graduate Center. I admit, however, I was the only one who ever taught the subject, and, sad to say, faculty apathy, perhaps even hostility, ended the effort. Yet the results were dramatic.

Although we spent some class time discussing ethical obligations and pedagogic principles, as well as developing sample syllabi and examinations, most of the hours were devoted to practice. Each of the approximately 15 students gave a series of short presentations to the class, after which the speaker received immediate feedback from me and the other students. If during the talk someone did not understand a term the speaker had used, that listener was expected immediately to raise a hand, thereby requesting an explanation.

At first, most of the participants were nervous as they stood before the audience. Some mumbled, talked too fast, laughed self-consciously, or stared at the ceiling, the chalkboard, or their notes, avoiding eye contact with those they were supposed to be addressing. Some made little attempt to interest their listeners in the subject, became lost in minutiae, or used technical terms without explaining them, thus provoking numerous raised hands. In short, these beginners displayed all the pedagogical shortcomings that turn too many college classrooms into scenes of apathy and confusion.

But whereas most instructors who communicate inadequately are never called to account, in this case weak presentations brought forth a series of constructive suggestions. Not only did these help the speaker, but they reinforced for all participants the elements of sound instruction and the precautions needed to avoid pedagogic pitfalls.

Soon noticeable improvements occurred. The students began to speak more slowly, motivate their audience, and organize the talks so that ideas were presented in a comprehensible sequence. Fewer hands were raised. Most remarkably, some students whose initial stage fright had made them seem somber or remote turned out, after becoming more at ease, to be engaging and even humorous.

Students whose presentations showed marked improvement received generous plaudits from the others, and the developing esprit de corps encouraged all to try to enhance their performance. Before long, most of the talks were more compelling, and the students who continued to struggle at least were conscious of the reasons for their lack of success.

After listening to each of the final presentations, all the students wrote evaluations that I later shared anonymously at personal conferences with each member of the class. Perhaps I can convey most effectively what we accomplished by quoting a sampling of these comments, each condensed but using the exact words of a respondent.

☐ Energetic, attention-grabbing, and polished presentation. Nice motivation, leading expertly to the topic to be discussed. Smooth interaction with students; handled comments well without distraction. Clear exposition of the issues at hand. Should avoid using notes too much. Should slow down a bit.

☐ Way too many "OKs". Too much looking at the board. No attempt at motivation. Many opportunities for discussion passed over. Though he asked us to raise our hands if we had a comment, there didn't seem to be any opportunities to do so.

☐ Powerful example used to motivate interest. The pace at times was a bit fast, perhaps because of nervousness. You asked questions but mostly answered them yourself. I think this made for a certain disengagement on the part of the class. It's hard to hold interest by just talking to the class. You need to connect to them.

- ☐ Became much more comfortable toward the end, warmed up, relaxed. You became able to use emphasis and tone to create drama, suspense, and interest. Nice, personable manner, and slow, clear pace.
- ☐ Don't look at the board like you're expecting it to do something. Make sure you're making eye contact with us. Your tone is calm and reassuring. Great use of example to build the point. You use the class and their answers well. It becomes a fun discussion.
- ☐ The pacing was a little fast in some places. Examples worked well, but I think that discussing them further, especially by asking students to participate at some point, would have worked even better. Overall, a lively and interesting presentation of a difficult topic.
- ☐ There's no motivation, no gateway into the issue. Way too attached to notes. Put them down. We desperately need examples. There's too much terminology tossed about, and nothing relevant or playful to tie it down. The main thrust of your attention is the board. Make the students your primary focus.
- ☐ Considerably more comfortable and casual than in previous presentations. Good use of humor to engage audience. Much better job of making eye contact and connecting with the class. A lot of information is covered a little too quickly. It would be a good idea to use the board to set up and outline and keep track of key terms. But overall so much better. Congratulations!

Aspiring college teachers who took such a course would never again suppose that teaching is easy, and their efforts to master essential pedagogic techniques would result in more effective instruction. Granted, no course is likely to turn a poor teacher into a great one. However, if taken during those formative years of graduate study, when individuals are most likely to welcome help, the advice provided can turn inaudible, unclear, or disorganized speakers into audible, clear, and organized ones. Most important, it can turn thoughtless instructors into thoughtful ones, a crucial step on the path toward more effective and responsible teaching.

One final note. During those years when the course was offered, chairs at departments where our students went to teach praised their performance. Once the course was abandoned, those same chairs began to complain about our students' inadequacy in the classroom. Such expressions of dissatisfaction, however, went unheeded by the many in our doctoral program who were focused entirely on research productivity and believed time spent on improving teaching was wasted. Never mind the students who suffered the consequences.

# Chapter 5

## *Why Graduate Schools Don't Have Reunions*

Last year I accompanied my wife to the 50th reunion of her medical school class at the Woman's Medical College of Pennsylvania, founded in 1850 and now consolidated into the Drexel University College of Medicine. That class was honored at commencement, and 15 of the original 58 graduates attended.

During the proceedings, I recalled that 2016 marked 50 years since I had received my doctoral degree from the Department of Philosophy at Columbia University. No one will be surprised to learn that a reunion from my era has never occurred. In fact, I have never heard of such an event at any graduate school. Why?

Whereas my wife was a member of a class that entered medical school and became a unit, working through shared rigors and graduating in step, my contemporaries did not progress together. All of us proceeded at our own pace and developed different projects while accommodating ourselves to the styles of those particular faculty with whom we interacted. Finally, as we struggled to complete our dissertations, most other students remained unaware of our headway. Those who finished did so at different times, while some became permanently stalled. In any case, few had a sense of belonging to a group.

As we in academia pursue our careers, merely attending graduate school together rarely creates a lasting bond. Instead, we build relationships through departmental affiliations or related research areas. Indeed, we are often unaware of where or under what circumstances any individual, however highly regarded, earned the doctorate.

For example, consider the path to a doctoral degree taken by renowned philosopher Harry Frankfurt. The story is found in his 2010 John Dewey Lecture. He recalls that after receiving a BA from Johns Hopkins University in 1949, he enrolled in Cornell University's prestigious graduate department but left after only two years. What happened? Here is his account:

> In my second year at Cornell, Professor Max Black chose me to be his assistant in his graduate Introduction to Symbolic Logic course, and I also assisted Professor Gregory Vlastos in his course on the History of Political Philosophy. However, my work as a student was evidently not very successful. Indeed, although I had not been aware that my performance as a student had actually been less than satisfactory, I was informed near the end of the year that my fellowship would not be renewed. This

made it financially impossible for me to return to Cornell. Accordingly, I went back to Johns Hopkins and continued my doctoral work there. After a bit more coursework—including seminars on Plato, on ethics, and on Whitehead—I wrote a doctoral dissertation entitled "The Essential Objectivity of What is Known" and was awarded the PhD (with distinction) in 1954.[1]

Almost everyone who attends graduate school could tell a personal story that, like Frankfurt's, includes mistreatment and setbacks. Whereas those in my wife's class enjoyed reminiscing, former doctoral students have little desire to recall battling through the thickets of their education. They are merely grateful the experience ended.

In sum, I don't expect an invitation to a graduate school reunion. Were such an event to occur, however, no doubt attendance would be sparse and conversation caustic.

## Note

1  Harry Frankfurt, "Reflections of My Career in Philosophy", in *Portraits of American Philosophy*, ed. Steven M. Cahn (Lanham, MD: Rowman & Littlefield, 2013), 112.

# Part II
# **Teaching**

# Chapter 6

## *Caring about Students*

A while ago, at a meeting of the American Philosophical Association, I passed a group of graduate students who were responding enthusiastically as one described a position for which he had just been interviewed. "It's a great job", he told his friends. "There's very little teaching, and I'll have plenty of time for my work". I wish someone had reminded him that, in fact, teaching *was* his work.

He might have responded, however, that many highly regarded professors only grudgingly give time or attention to the classroom. Instead, they concentrate on their own scholarship.

In doing so, they reflect a theme of academic life that I have mentioned previously: Publication is the key to advancement. The time you devote to research redounds to your benefit; the concern you show students rarely does.

This attitude is reinforced by various academic practices. For example, when deciding about salary, support, promotion, or tenure, administrators almost always favor success in publishing over success in teaching. After all, the celebrated scholar focuses attention on the institution whereas even the most outstanding of instructors is at best a local celebrity, legendary perhaps on campus but unknown outside its gates.

Yet despite the absence of encouragement, more professors than might be supposed are deeply concerned with whether their students become interested in the subject, grasp assigned readings, understand explanations in class, and view as reasonable assignments, examinations, and grades. Why do these instructors care about such pedagogical matters?

Answers to the question will vary, depending on whether appeal is made to an ethics of duties, consequences, or virtues, but in any case, teaching has a moral dimension, for instructors have the capacity to help or harm others.

Let's return to a variation on the story with which I began. Suppose you go to a doctor's office and overhear the physicians discussing with zest the possibility that one of them might be fortunate enough to obtain a laboratory position that would not involve seeing any patients. As you listen, you realize that these practitioners are concerned primarily with their own research, not with your personal medical problems. In such circumstances most of us would seek doctors who are more eager to provide help. Likewise, students respond negatively to any professor who by word or deed reflects the attitude that teaching is merely a distraction from the essence of the academic enterprise.

Nevertheless, a colleague might ask skeptically, "Why should I put effort into classes when doing so doesn't advance my career?" Here is a version of the familiar challenge, "Why should I be moral?" Whatever the reply, if professors don't care about their students, then those students are the losers.

# Chapter 7

## *Teaching All the Students*

Years ago, the department of which I was then a member invited to campus a promising candidate for a faculty position. He had been highly recommended based in part on his purported pedagogical skills, but after listening to him present a convoluted talk, I had doubts. Later, as he recounted his success in teaching introductory philosophy, I asked him to estimate the percentage of students in the class who understood his lectures. "Definitely half", he replied proudly. When I inquired about the other half, he answered that they were not philosophically sophisticated enough to follow the arguments. No wonder, given that department's commitment to excellence in teaching, he was not offered a position.

We all recognize that some students are stronger than others, and often the temptation is to focus on the standouts. The aim of teaching, however, is not to bring enjoyment to instructors but to enlighten students. And although some are difficult to reach, all who are trying to learn should be offered help in doing so. Remember, every student has registered for the class and deserves attention. Furthermore, most have the necessary ability to succeed, assuming their instructor is capable and cares about their progress.

Concern for all students is compatible with reaching out to the strongest, perhaps by offering them in-class challenges or extra-credit assignments. In truth, though, the talented do not need more help than others. Do you suppose Plato was worried whether he could keep Aristotle's attention?

While few professors underestimate how much their students are learning, many instructors overestimate. They are dismayed when examination papers display egregious misunderstanding, and are apt to disparage students whose work contains simple errors. A likely explanation for the phenomenon, however, is that the instruction was inadequate. Professors dissatisfied with the performance of their students may take refuge in supposing that the material lies beyond their grasp, but as Tamar Szabó Gendler, dean of the Faculty of Arts and Sciences at Yale University, once remarked to me, any subject can be explained successfully if you know how.

The challenge of effective teaching is to reach not only students who come to class with enthusiasm and continually raise their hands to participate. Rather, the key is whether you can appeal to students who arrive in class with little interest and seemingly limited talents. The crucial question is: Can you excite these students about the material and enhance their knowledge and skills?

Admittedly, doing so is difficult. Yet good teachers sometimes succeed, and great teachers often do. Granted, even the finest instructors fail occasionally, but in that case they are likely to express dissatisfaction not with their students but with themselves.

At an interview, when candidates are asked about the extent of their success in the classroom, I have little confidence in anyone who replies, "I don't think too much about teaching, but mine's okay". Rather, I hope to hear, "I believe I reach the students, but I'm always trying to improve". The most unsatisfying answer, which I have heard too often, is "I work well with good students". In that case, I am always tempted to respond, "Who doesn't?"

# Chapter 8

## *How Teachers Succeed*

Knowing a subject and knowing how to teach it effectively are quite different. No doubt you remember that in school you experienced much ineffective instruction. The problem was not primarily that the teachers were uninformed about the subject but that they did not know how to engage students. Information was presented, but the process was boring, confusing, or unsatisfying. Yet some of your teachers found ways to lead students in grasping appropriate subject matter while arousing appreciation for it.

Now the crucial question is: What do successful teachers have in common that others lack? The answer is not a mysterious *je ne sais quoi* but attention to three strategic elements that lead to success.

The first is commonly referred to as "motivation". Without it, a class stagnates. After all, how long will you watch a movie that does nothing to capture your attention? Or read a novel that begins with a situation of no interest? The slower the start, the more difficult to generate enthusiasm. At best, the audience allows you a few minutes without much action. The same with teaching.

Here is an example that I offer not because of its profundity but simply because I found that it worked with students. (I should add that while my own success in the classroom does not match that achieved by some others I have known, I take second place to no one in my admiration for the magic they perform in turning classrooms into scenes of inspiration.)

In teaching introductory philosophy I usually include John Stuart Mill's account of the case for free thought and discussion in his classic work *On Liberty*.[1] Although I assign relevant pages for preparatory reading, I don't begin the class by referring to Mill or his book. Rather, I ask students to suppose that as they entered the building they saw a table where passersby were being urged to "sign the petition". Imagine, I continue, that you had strolled over to learn more and were urged to add your name to a letter addressed to the administration, demanding that an invited speaker with a well-documented record of having expressed racist and sexist views not be allowed to appear. Would you sign?

Most are sure they would, and the few holdouts quickly lose confidence in their position as others in the class accuse them of insensitivity to those who are the targets of prejudice. At that point I inquire: "Would John Stuart Mill sign the petition?" Suddenly the students recognize the significance of Mill's defense of free expression, and they agree that Mill would not support the effort to block the talk. "Why not?" I ask, and the discussion proceeds apace.

What such a motivational device does is make apparent the connections between seemingly esoteric material and the students' own sphere of experience, so that the subject itself becomes their personal concern. I know of no formula for developing effective motivational devices, which is one reason why teaching is an art. Yet whether the instructor begins by offering a striking thesis, an engaging anecdote, or a stimulating puzzle, a weak attempt to motivate will be better than none.

Even with a motivated student, though, a successful teacher needs to know how to take advantage of such interest. A key element is organization, presenting material in a sequence that promotes understanding.

To grasp the challenge, imagine trying to explain baseball to a person unfamiliar with the sport. Where would you begin? With the roles of the pitcher and catcher? How about the calling of balls and strikes? Or the location of the bases, how to score runs, or the ways outs can be made? The fundamental difficulty is that all these starting points presume knowledge of some of the others. How, then, can you break the circle of intertwining concepts and make the subject accessible?

Consider the following attempt: "In playing baseball you try to score runs. Only the team to whom the ball is pitched can score. You run around the bases and try to avoid outs. Three strikes and you're out. The game has nine innings".

This attempt at teaching is a failure. Not that any of the statements is false. Each is true yet not only disconnected from the previous ones but also presuming knowledge the listener doesn't possess.

The first statement refers to "runs", but the learner hasn't been told how a run is scored. The second statement refers to a ball being "pitched", but the role of the pitcher hasn't been explained. The remaining statements refer to "bases", "outs"," "strikes", and "innings", but none of the terms has been put in context. In short, if you don't already understand baseball, you won't learn much from this explanation. In other words, a presentation can be factual yet not pedagogically well organized. (Incidentally, one strategy to consider would be beginning with the diagram of a baseball field.)

Even a motivated and well-organized presentation, however, will be unsuccessful if not clear.

One problem is speaking too quickly. No matter what your content, if you speak too rapidly, you won't be understood. Indeed, the most obvious sign of a poor lecturer is rushing. When those who are inexperienced come to a podium, they hardly ever speak at a proper pace. With a genuine orator, however, sentences come slowly. No student will ever object to a teacher's speaking too deliberately, but many will complain if words cascade.

Another problem is using terminology the audience doesn't understand. If I remark that for a year I worked at the NEH, which has a different mission from the NEA and is unconnected to the DOJ, Washington insiders will know that I am referring to the National Endowment for the Humanities, the National Endowment for the Arts, and the Department of Justice, but others will be lost. Should they know these acronyms? Maybe; maybe not. Either way, if many are unfamiliar with them, that situation is reason enough not to use them without explanation.

Imagine listening to an instructor in an introductory course who says, "To paraphrase the author of *The Pastorals*, a sparse supply of cognition is a minatory entity". Few in any class are likely to understand this remark. If the problem is pointed out to the speaker, the irritated reply may be, "It's obvious that I'm referring to Alexander Pope". "But who", a student might ask, "is Alexander Pope?" At this point, the instructor is likely to burst out with frustration: "How can you not know?" Perhaps needless to say, this person is not cut out to be a teacher. And even if the students were told that Pope was a celebrated early eighteenth-century English poet, they probably still would not realize that the teacher was paraphrasing Pope's line, "A little learning is a dangerous thing", which, in fact, may itself be unknown to many.

And why use the word "minatory"? Hardly anyone will be aware of its meaning, which is derived from the Latin word *minari*, meaning "to threaten". Yet inept teachers proceed in such confusing ways all the time.

Another reason for lack of clarity is omitting steps in reasoning. Suppose an instructor of first-year students who need to brush up on algebra says, "Given that

17 − 11 = 3x, we know that 2x = 4". Many students in the class will not follow the reasoning. The teacher has failed to take the time to explain how the first equation proves that x = 2, thus 2 × 2 = 4.

The teacher might respond that such reasoning is obvious. Well, it may be obvious to the teacher but not to all the students, and their understanding should be the instructor's focus.

But can't you omit what seems apparent? The question brings to mind an incident, reported by a number of witnesses, involving Willard Van Orman Quine, one of the greatest logicians of the twentieth century and a professor of philosophy at Harvard University. His textbook on symbolic logic was widely used, and although he didn't relish teaching the subject, he was occasionally asked to do so. Once in such a course, after Quine wrote a proof on the board, a student raised his hand and asked impatiently, "Why bother writing out that proof? It's obvious". To which Quine replied, "Young man, this entire course is obvious".

In an introductory course, everything taught may be obvious—obvious to the teacher but not to the students. The same may sometimes be true in a graduate seminar.

To sum up, when you discover an instructor who motivates the class, organizes the material, and presents it clearly, you have found a successful teacher. Incidentally, the same principles apply whether the class is composed of fifth graders, high schoolers, undergraduates, or PhD candidates.

Show me a terrific elementary school teacher, and I'll show you someone who, with specialist study, could become an outstanding instructor at the collegiate level. Show me a boring college professor, and I'll show you someone who would be equally tiresome to a class of ten-year-olds. The difference is that when youngsters are not engaged, they are likely to disrupt the proceedings. Adults merely fall asleep.

## Note

1 John Stuart Mill, *On Liberty*, with introduction and study guide by C. L. Ten and annotations by Steven M. Cahn (Lanham, MD: Rowman & Littlefield, 2005).

# Chapter 9

## *Teaching and Testing*

One aspect of teaching disliked by both students and teachers is examinations. For students they are the stuff of nightmares; for teachers they result in stacks of papers requiring correction and grading. Thus the question arises: Why not dispense with tests?

The answer is that, carefully prepared, they serve important purposes. First, an exam provides the opportunity for students to discover the scope and depth of their understanding. To speak glibly about a subject is not nearly as indicative of one's knowledge as to reply without prompting to pertinent questions and commit those answers to paper so they can be scrutinized.

Students, though, are not the only ones tested by exams. Another purpose they serve is providing teachers with the opportunity to assess the effectiveness of their instruction. Through analyzing the results of tests, teachers can learn how they have succeeded and where they have failed.

An additional value to examinations is the time spent preparing for them. Because questions are not known beforehand, students need to undertake a thorough study of all the material and anticipate what may be asked. In doing so, they are led to analyze and synthesize material, thereby enhancing their control of it.

Term papers have their own worth but are not substitutes for an examination. In researching papers, students need master only those parts of the course bearing directly on the chosen topic. Suppose you take a course in the American political system and are asked to learn the roles of the executive, legislative, and judicial branches of the United States government. If you write a term paper on the Department of Education, you may do so without showing mastery of much of the course material. Only an examination will cover all the ground.

In this connection, consider a student who came to see me after having received a C on her test. She was disappointed, especially because, as she explained, she had always been an A student. I asked whether she had studied as hard for this exam as for previous ones, but to my surprise she told me that she had never before taken an examination. She had gone to a secondary school where tests were considered outmoded, then her first two collegiate years were spent at a school that had substituted term papers for exams. I asked whether she thought her learning had been helped or hindered by their absence. She replied that she had always thought that avoiding them had been to her advantage, but she now realized that her grasp of material had been flimsy. She had never learned a body of material thoroughly enough to draw on it at will and utilize it effectively whenever needed. In short, she never had received the benefits of studying for an exam.

But if examinations are so beneficial, what are the arguments against them?

First, some say that exams do not provide a sound basis for evaluating a student's achievement. After all, they require a student to demonstrate knowledge under challenging conditions, answering a restricted set of questions within a limited time, thus causing pressure that prevents many from doing their best work.

This line of argument, however, overlooks that pressure exists whenever anyone attempts to prove competence to experts. For example, a violinist feels pressure when auditioning for an orchestral position. Tension is inherent in such situations because experts have high standards that are challenging to meet and you need to meet them at an appointed time. The golfer who appears skillful at the practice tee but plays poorly on the course lacks effective control of the requisite skills. Similarly, students who sound informed in conversation but perform poorly in exams lack command of their subject. Thus the pressure of examinations does not invalidate but confirms the significance of the results.

A second criticism is that exams inhibit students' independence, discouraging them from pursuing their own interests and instead forcing the study of materials chosen by the instructor.

Why assume, though, that mastering a subject involves only learning those aspects you happen to find interesting? For example, knowing American history involves knowing all periods, not just the Civil War or the New Deal. You may not be interested in the Colonial age, but if you claim expertise in American history, you're expected to know it all. And the teacher is your guide to identifying the important aspects of a subject. Such perspective is not limiting but liberating, removing barriers to understanding and making possible more independent thinking.

A final criticism of examinations is that they stifle creativity, emphasizing the mindless reiteration of facts instead of encouraging imaginative thinking. Thus exams are said to impede rather than promote learning.

But this line of attack is mistaken for two reasons. First, only poor exams emphasize learning by rote. Good ones place familiar material in a somewhat unfamiliar light and lead students to make valuable connections in their thinking.

Second, the mastery of any field requires control of relevant information and skills. As Whitehead wrote, "There is no getting away from the fact that things have been found out, and that to be effective in the modern world you must have a store of definite acquirement of the best practice. To write poetry you must study metre; and to build bridges you must be learned in the strength of material. Even the Hebrew prophets had learned to write, probably in those days requiring no mean effort.

The untutored art of genius is—in the words of the Prayer Book—a vain thing, fondly invented".[1]

Imaginative thinking does not flow from those ignorant of fundamental information, and examinations reveal whether you know the basics. Hence testing, rather than stifling creativity, provides a framework in which it can flourish.

Finally, here is an example from my own experience. For many years I taught a graduate course in political philosophy, covering the work of major historical authors, including Plato, Aristotle, Hobbes, Locke, Rousseau, and Mill. Their writings are among the foundations of the field, and I wanted each student to master them. To encourage this result, I gave mid-term and final exams that called for detailed knowledge of the key texts. I explained that the mid-term was a diagnostic tool that students could use to assess their work. After the test was given, I returned the papers in the next class and reviewed them question by question, explaining the correct answers and indicating where in our anthology they could be found.

I did not, however, anticipate what happened next. The students voluntarily formed study groups to prepare for the final examination, quizzing one another to gain mastery of these crucial works. Later, they reported how much they had learned and how pleased they were to have acquired such a firm grasp of the fundamental texts of political philosophy.

In short, examinations are neither good nor bad, but they are one tool in the teacher's kit. If prepared properly and used appropriately, they are a powerful pedagogical device that can encourage and assess learning.

## Note

1   Alfred North Whitehead, *The Aims of Education and Other Essays* (New York: The Free Press, 1967), 34.

# Chapter 10

## *Teaching and Grading*

Many teachers are uncomfortable with grades, viewing them as inherently inaccurate devices that in attempting to measure people, only traumatize and dehumanize them. This concern, however, is a tangle of misconceptions.

A grade represents an expert's judgment of the quality of a student's work in a specific course. As such, it can serve not only to determine whether students are making satisfactory progress or earning academic honors but also to aid students themselves in judging their past efforts and formulating their future plans.

Would these functions be better served if, as some have suggested, grades were replaced by letters of evaluation? In addition to the impracticality of a professor's writing hundreds of individual comments and evaluators reading thousands, the value of such letters would be severely limited if they didn't include specific indications of students' levels of performance—in other words, grades. Otherwise, the letters would be more likely to reveal the teachers' literary styles than the students' academic accomplishments. Remarks one instructor considers high praise may be used indiscriminately by another, whereas comments intended as mild commendation might be mistaken as tempered criticism.

While a piece of work would not necessarily be graded identically by all specialists, members of the same department usually agree whether a student's performance has been outstanding, good, fair, poor, or unsatisfactory, the levels of achievement typically symbolized by A through F. Granted, experts sometimes disagree, but in doing so they do not obliterate the distinction between their knowledgeable judgments and a novice's uninformed impressions.

What of the oft-repeated charge that grades are impersonal devices that reduce people to letters of the alphabet? That criticism is misguided. A grade is not a measure of a person but of a person's level of achievement in a particular course. A student who receives a C in introductory philosophy is not a C person with a C personality or C moral character but one whose performance in introductory philosophy was acceptable but in no way distinguished. Perhaps the student will do much better in later courses and even excel at philosophy, but this first try was not highly successful.

Whether grades are fair, however, depends on a teacher's conscientiousness in assigning them. One potential misuse is to award grades on bases other than a student's level of achievement. Irrelevant criteria include a student's gender, race, nationality, physical appearance, dress, personality, attitudes, innate capacities, and previous academic record. None of these factors should even be considered in deciding a student's grade. Performance in the course should be the only criterion.

If an A in symbolic logic might mean that the student tried hard, came from an impoverished community, or displayed an ingratiating personality, then the A is hopelessly ambiguous and serves no purpose. If, on the other hand, the grade signifies that the student has a firm grasp of the essentials of symbolic logic, then the message is clear.

The most effective means for ensuring that no extraneous factors enter into grading is for the instructor to make clear at the beginning of the term how final grades will be determined. How much will the final examination count? How about the papers and other short assignments? Will a student's participation be a factor? Answering these questions at the outset enables students to concentrate their energies on the most important aspects of the course, not waste time speculating about the instructor's intentions.

Yet if the announced system is unnecessarily complicated, it can distort the purpose of the course. For example, if the teacher announces that to receive an A you need to accumulate 965 points out of 1000 and the final exam is worth 350, each of the other two exams is worth 120, each of the two papers is worth 140, and class discussion is worth 130, the class has taken on the elements of a complicated game show. The rule of thumb is: Explain your grading system but keep matters simple.

The most common misuse of the grading system is the practice commonly referred to as "grading on a curve". The essence of this scheme is for the instructor to decide before the course begins what percentage of students will receive each grade. This method may produce aesthetically pleasing designs on a graph but is nevertheless conceptually confused. While a student's achievement should be judged in the light of reasonable expectations, these do not depend on such haphazard circumstances as the mix of students who happen to be taking the course concurrently.

Consider the plight of a student who earns an 80 on an examination but receives a D because most classmates scored higher. Yet the following semester in the same course, another earns an 80 with the same answers and receives an A because this time almost all classmates scored lower. Two students, identical work, different grades: the system is patently unfair.

Years ago, I overheard a student complain to the instructor about receiving a B. This nationally known scholar responded sympathetically but explained with regret that all the As were taken. His philosophical skills far exceeded his pedagogic wisdom.

Why do too many instructors resort to this approach? Because by doing so they avoid responsibility for determining the level of work each grade represents. They are also free to construct examinations without concern for skewed results, because even if the highest grade is 30 out of 100, grading on a curve will yield apparently acceptable consequences. Yet the appearance is deceiving because rank in class will have been confused with mastery of the subject. The procrustean practice of grading on a curve rests on this muddle and should be abandoned (although inept teaching or badly constructed examinations should not be allowed to yield unconscionably low grades).

A different distortion of the grading system, rare nowadays, is an unwillingness to award high grades. Instructors who adopt this attitude take pride in rigor. But just as a third-grade student who receives an A in mathematics need not be the equal of Isaac Newton, so a freshman may deserve an A without being the philosophical equal of Aristotle. Receiving an A in an introductory course does not signify that a student has mastered philosophy, only that, judged by reasonable expectations, the student has done excellent work. An instructor who rarely awards high grades is failing to distinguish good from poor performance. Doing so does not uphold academic standards but only misinterprets the grading symbols, thereby undermining their appropriate functions.

A more common misuse of the grading system is the reluctance to award low grades, a practice popularly known as "grade inflation". It results from the unwillingness of professors to give students the bad news that they have not done as well as they might have hoped. Yet maintaining academic standards rests on the willingness of professors to tell the truth. Understandably, some are concerned about the possible injustice of giving their own students realistic grades while other students receive inflated ones. The solution, adopted at some colleges, is for transcripts to include not only a student's course grade but also the average grade for all students in the course. In this way, grade inflation is publicly exposed and unfairness dissipated. In any case, each instructor who inflates grades adds to the problem.

Yet awarding grades also calls for a sense of fair play. Consider a teacher I knew who gave relatively easy exams throughout the semester, thereby leading students to believe they were doing well. The final examination, however, was vastly more difficult, and many students were shocked and angered to receive low grades for the course. Clearly, this instructor misled and harmed his students. He was like a storeowner who announces a major sale but applies low prices only to a few rarely sought items.

After all, ethics applies not only to physicians, nurses, lawyers, business managers, journalists, and engineers but also to teachers. They, too, can lie, mislead, and fail to fulfill all manner of professional responsibilities. Indeed, classrooms are no more free of misconduct than hospitals, courts, or boardrooms.[1]

Grading is especially sensitive to mishandling because assessments are done privately and results are not easily challenged. Teachers, therefore, need to be aware of this pitfall and make every effort to treat students equitably.

## Note

1 For an extended discussion of the topic, see Steven M. Cahn, *Saints and Scamps: Ethics in Academia*, 25th Anniversary Edition (Lanham, MD: Rowman & Littlefield, 2011).

# Chapter 11

## *Improving Teaching*

All those who seek to teach effectively welcome advice on how to enhance classroom skills. Let me offer one suggestion.

When we write a paper, we typically show a draft to at least one of our colleagues. We find someone whose philosophical judgment we trust and who offers criticism in a constructive spirit. Then we share our work and almost always benefit.

Why not follow the same procedure with teaching? Find a sympathetic colleague who takes teaching seriously and show that person a draft of your syllabus. Then adjust it in accord with any reaction you find helpful.

Furthermore, once the course begins, invite that colleague to attend a session and share thoughts on the proceedings. The observer should sit in the back of the room and not take any role (participation impedes disinterested evaluation) but afterwards should discuss with you all aspects of the session: how a question was well put, how discussion may have gone off the track, whether you were audible, whether your writing on the chalkboard was visible, how a difficult concept might have been presented more clearly, or how an idea explained in one context might have been applied in another. The aim is not to interfere with your distinctive teaching style but to enhance it.

Three major pitfalls should always be of concern:

1. Did you neglect to interest students in the subject by not connecting the course material and the students' own experience?
2. Did you confuse students by either assuming background knowledge they lacked or proceeding too quickly for them to follow the reasoning?
3. Did you caricature your intellectual opponents, failing to explain as clearly as possible why they disagree with you?

Of course, if you believe for any reason that a colleague does not possess the know-how or willingness to offer constructive criticism, don't invite that person. Just as you would not ask for help on a paper from someone ill suited to the task, the same is true for requesting feedback on teaching.

Yet why would someone agree to spend time and effort to attend your class, then sit with you afterwards to provide a review? Because you will do the same in return.

Such exchange visits are not formal observations intended to serve as part of a promotion or tenure review. Rather, they are informal arrangements meant to benefit both you and your colleague. Admittedly, you may not agree with every suggestion offered, but almost surely you will learn something of value from the reactions of an informed observer who brings a different perspective to your efforts.

I recognize that many instructors object to teaching in the presence of colleagues, but almost all faculty welcome as guests auditors, friends or relatives of students, and even members of other departments. Why, then, be reluctant to invite a knowledgeable and sympathetic commentator who can offer useful advice?

Admittedly, this practice is not a panacea. More often than not, however, it will be productive and may on occasion prove revelatory.

# Chapter 12

## *Evaluating Teaching*

Given that faculty are expected to guide learning, their authority to do so should be protected. One subtle threat is posed by the widespread practice of judging an instructor's pedagogic skill primarily on the basis of evaluations prepared by students.

The practice began in the 1960s when a few enterprising undergraduates distributed light-hearted compilations intended to aid those registering for courses by providing tips about the more and less effective members of the faculty. A decade later, these informal reactions had been transformed into complex statistics, obtained by formal procedures and relied on heavily by administrators to help decide an instructor's reappointment, promotion, and tenure.

The rationale for instituting such a system was that when faculty fail to fulfill their obligations, students suffer the consequences. Shouldn't students, therefore, have a strong voice in evaluating faculty?

This line of reasoning is fallacious. When airplane pilots fail to fulfill their obligations, passengers often suffer the consequences, but passengers should not have a strong voice in evaluating pilots. A plane has a rough landing. Was the pilot at fault? Simply being a passenger does not enable one to know.

Some proponents of student ratings have argued that learners are the best evaluators of their own responses, drawing an analogy to the restaurant patron who is a better judge of the food than the chef. But while those who eat know how the food tastes, its nutritional benefit is judged most reliably by a nutritionist, just as educational value is best judged by an educator.

Students, by definition, have not mastered the subject they are studying; hence they are in poor position to judge how well it is being taught. Perhaps they find a concept challenging. Is the instructor to blame, or is the difficulty intrinsic to the material?

Granted, students are a convenient source for easily verifiable matters such as whether teachers hold class regularly, return examinations without delay, provide detailed comments on term papers, and appear at announced office hours. Students, however, are not in a position to know whether faculty are knowledgeable or their presentations reliable.

Consider this question that appeared on a widely used evaluation form: "Does the instructor discuss recent developments in the field?" How are students expected to know the source of the information a teacher offers? Even if something is described to them as a recent development in the field, they are still in the dark as to whether that material is either recent or significant.

Some years ago an experiment was carried out under controlled conditions to test the hypothesis that learners can be seriously mistaken about their instructor's competence. A distinguished-looking professional actor with an authoritative manner (real name: Michael Fox) was selected to present a lecture to several groups of educators. They were told they would be hearing a talk by Dr. Myron L. Fox, an expert on the application of mathematics to human behavior. His address was titled "Mathematical Game Theory as Applied to Physician Education". The actor was coached "to present his topic and conduct his question-and-answer period with an excessive use of double talk, neologies, non sequiturs, and contradictory statements. All this was to be interspersed with parenthetical and meaningless references to unrelated topics".

At the end of the one-hour lecture and subsequent half-hour discussion, a questionnaire was distributed to the listeners, inquiring what they thought of Dr. Fox. Here are some responses:

> Excellent presentation, enjoyed listening.
> Has warm manner. Good flow, seems enthusiastic.
> Lively examples. Extremely articulate.
> Good analysis of subject that has been personally studied before.
> He was certainly captivating. Knowledgeable.

My favorite reply was offered by one participant who found the presentation "too intellectual". Most important, all the listeners had many more favorable than unfavorable responses and not one saw through the hoax. The authors' conclusion was that "students' satisfaction with learning may represent little more than the illusion of having learned".[1]

Admittedly, student ratings yield quantifiable results that can easily be given the appearance of exactitude. For example, I have before me a computer-generated spreadsheet, typical of those provided each semester to faculty at many colleges. It indicates that in a particular course, for "Mastery of Style" the instructor scored 4.85 (on a scale of 1 to 5). The average for instructors for all sections of the course was 4.67; for all courses in the department, the average was 4.60; and for all courses in the school, the average was 4.62. Whatever trust the credulous might place in such pseudo-precise statistics, note that the course in which this instructor received a superior rating was English composition.

Sending such data to faculty members with the understanding that their scores will play a significant role in personnel decisions is demeaning to all involved.

Furthermore, evaluating an instructor primarily on the basis of student opinion is not only inappropriate but also dangerous. As philosopher Charles Frankel observed, "Teaching is a professional relationship, not a popularity contest. To invite students to participate in the selection or promotion of their teachers…exposes the teacher to intimidation".[2] No professor should be put in a position in which advantage is gained by granting students favors in exchange for their support.

Admittedly, some educational researchers have concluded that student evaluations, viewed in proper perspective, can provide useful information. The crucial insight, however, supported by numerous studies, is that such evaluations always need to be considered in the context of peer evaluations. Otherwise, as one researcher concluded long ago and numerous others have since confirmed, institutions are "flying blind".[3]

Corporate executives judge other corporate executives to decide promotions in the company, and attorneys judge other attorneys to decide partnerships in the law firm. Likewise, professors should judge other professors to decide matters such as reappointment, promotion, and tenure. Indeed, no professionals should shirk the responsibility of judging their colleagues. To do so is not only inappropriate but inimical to the interests of those supposed to be served. After all, if a quack is practicing surgery in a hospital, who is to blame, the patients or the other physicians? If an incompetent is lecturing at a university, the ones at fault are not the students but the other professors. They are responsible for systematically observing classes and gaining insight into what is occurring.

Faculty rightfully claim authority in the academic sphere. When the time comes for evaluating teaching, they should not abandon their duty.

# Notes

1   Donald H. Naftulin, John E. Ware, Jr., and Frank A. Donnelly,
    "The Doctor Fox Lecture: A Paradigm of Educational
    Seduction", *Journal of Medical Education* 48 (1973), 630–635.
    Footage of the lecture is available on YouTube.
2   Charles Frankel, *Education and the Barricades* (New York:
    Norton, 1968), 30–31.
3   Charles B. Schultz, "Some Limits to the Validity and Usefulness
    of Student Rating of Teachers: An Argument for Caution",
    *Educational Research Quarterly* 3 (1978), 12–27.

# Part III
# Departments

# Chapter 13

## *Departmental Life*

A professor's appointment is not only to a school's faculty but also to a particular department, and every one, like a family, is unique. To paraphrase the opening of *Anna Karenina*, all happy departments are alike, but each unhappy department is unhappy in its own fashion.

The ideal is a friendly department where colleagues who might disagree intellectually nevertheless provide mutual support, share pedagogical advice, comment on one another's scholarly papers, and work together for the common good. In such an atmosphere, the welfare of students is treated as of prime importance, and they are able to pursue their studies without the detrimental effects of personal animosities among the faculty.

Yet other departments are filled with discord. In one, authoritarian rule leads to resentment and eventual rebellion, whereas in another infirm leadership results in anarchy. Some are beset by hostile factions engaged in a variety of personal, political, or scholarly disputes. Although the origins of such battles may be shrouded in ancient history, the feuds live on and continue to divide members. In such struggles, students are typically used as pawns and their academic needs are virtually forgotten.

The departmental cast of characters includes those who stress research, those who focus on teaching, those who perform much school service, and some who excel in two or even all three areas. Unfortunately, we may also find members who are barely adequate in any.

I myself have had as colleagues such memorable figures as a crusty old-timer with few publications who taught the same courses with the exact same reading lists for decades; a fading scholar whose alcoholism began to overshadow his considerable academic achievements; a successful writer and teacher who became disengaged from departmental responsibilities and left to join the faculty at another school in order to obtain a better pension; a prolific scholar who was eventually consumed by debauchery; a sincere but ineffective teacher without scholarly ambition who inherited a fortune and lost interest in academic pursuits; a fine scholar and strong teacher whose work was gradually overwhelmed by a passion for radical politics; and a beginner who published papers in prestigious journals but found academic life not to his liking and embarked instead on a promising career as a lawyer.

A significant complication is that faculty in the same department may approach their common discipline with strikingly different interests and methodologies. I recall an incident involving a celebrated analytic philosopher who entered an elevator in his office building and found himself alone with an equally famous, old-time historian of ideas. They had never met before and exchanged not a word until coming to their common floor, then going separate ways. As the analytic philosopher later remarked, "I couldn't think of anything to say to him".

How much does an expert in Chaucer share with another professor of English who specializes in Faulkner? These two may reside in the same department yet have little in common.

Students often imagine that, although they find difficulty in dealing with certain professors, faculty members themselves get along amiably. Nothing could be further from the truth. Departments can be filled with animosities, and professors may be glad they do not have to study with certain colleagues whose work they consider inadequate and whose personalities they find grating.

These tensions come to the fore in departmental meetings. Some might suppose that professors whose lives center on reasoned discussion would behave in exemplary fashion at academic meetings. Actually, remarkably few professors are able to transfer their scholarly skills to practical issues. Just present the group with a real-life problem, and the meeting is apt to turn into a mélange of reminiscences, irrelevancies, and impracticalities. Rarely can consensus be reached and even then likely fails to do justice to the complexities of the problem. Once in a while, however, a faculty member demonstrates the ability to think clearly and offer realistic solutions. That person is apt to become the departmental chair and, if willing, may be on track to a career in administration.

An academic once remarked that his colleagues possess "cognitive abilities of a special sort, which are…extremely sophisticated *relative* to the population norm".[1] I can only suppose he had never witnessed a departmental meeting.

## Note

1 Neil Levy, "Downshifting and Meaning in Life", *Ratio* 18, no. 2 (2005), 187–188.

# Chapter 14

## *Faculty Appointments*

Perhaps no process puts more strain on a department than the search for a new colleague. Indeed, the effort can intensify friction or create it where none existed.

The procedure, though, is familiar. Once a department is informed that it can make an appointment, the announcement of the position needs to be developed. The question then arises as to which subfields, if any, will be given prominence in the search. Ideally, the decision should reflect fair assessment of the department's needs. Too often, however, that criterion is ignored.

Imagine a music department that has four members teaching the history of Western music. Let us designate them as $A$, $B$, $C$, and $D$. $A$ teaches Renaissance music; $B$ specializes in the baroque age, particularly J. S. Bach; $C$ focuses on the classical period, especially Beethoven, and $D$ teaches music of the twentieth and twenty-first centuries. What is missing?

A neutral observer would immediately recognize a crucial gap: composers of the romantic era, including Brahms and Wagner.

That era, however, may *not* be the department's first priority. Consider how the discussion might proceed:

A "I'm supposed to cover all of Renaissance music, but I focus on the early period. We need someone for the middle and late."

B "While my work is centered on Bach, there's so much more in the baroque. Let's add someone who can handle it. The nineteenth century is important, but I haven't heard much call from students for Tchaikovsky."

C "Recently, I've been concentrating on Beethoven's quartets. How about someone who can delve into Haydn and Mozart? We can also use someone who could teach the year-long survey in the history of music."

D "Contemporary music is so varied that we need another person to do it justice. I have a friend from graduate school who works in electronic music and would be a terrific colleague."

The pattern is clear. Every member hopes to use the appointment to advance personal interests.

Here is commentary to help explain the discussion.

*A*, the historian of the Renaissance, seeks a colleague with similar interests so as to have someone at hand for discussion and assistance. Rather than saying so, however, *A* stresses differences between the early and later Renaissance, then claims that the department needs a specialist in both. The problem, of course, is that any subject can be divided into smaller units and the argument made that each unit needs coverage. We might term this strategy "divide and augment".

Suppose, for instance, instead of one professor doing Shakespeare, we split the field into tragedies, histories, comedies, and romances, then argue for specialists in each area. And how about someone to cover Shakespeare's sonnets? Suddenly five professors are teaching Shakespeare. In a large department, multiple scholars for a single area might be reasonable, but this small program has room for only one historian of Renaissance music.

*B*, the historian of baroque music, also uses the "divide and augment" strategy, followed by an appeal to lack of student interest in nineteenth-century music. But why expect students to urge that a subject they have never studied should be taught? If baroque music were not in the curriculum, would students complain?

*C*, the scholar of the classical period, wants to focus on Beethoven and also seeks someone to teach the survey of music history that requires extensive preparation and covers materials outside any one instructor's interests. *C* proposes that the members of the department avoid that demanding assignment by giving it to a newcomer.

*D*, the contemporary music scholar, uses the "divide and augment" strategy, then adds what might be labelled the "I have a friend" approach. This maneuver typically leads a professor to overrate pals, then become angry if colleagues do not share this inflated view. To avoid the problem, all department members should agree that in considering candidates, no one is under any obligation to be favorably disposed toward anyone else's friend. All subsequent discussion of candidates should be untarnished by any reference to personal attachments, and anyone suggesting a friend should stay out of the discussion of that candidate. Failure to do so is one of the most common reasons for unfortunate appointments.

Once the four members of the department present their opinions, the discussion usually turns repetitive and possibly unpleasant, as each one reiterates ever more forcefully already-stated positions. In accord with academic manners, however, attacks are never launched against the value of anyone else's research area but instead framed as defenses of one's own. How to break the impasse?

One solution calls for the advertisement to include a list of specializations sought: the later Renaissance, the baroque age, Haydn and Mozart, the nineteenth century, and electronic music. That approach will likely satisfy the four members but appear strange to potential candidates who will wonder why the department has such an unusual collection of priorities.

Here an effective dean might step in and insist that the complex advertisement be sharpened. How might the department react to the dean's objection? A common move is to declare that the search will seek the best person, regardless of field. This step might temporarily satisfy all involved but down the road produces poor results.

The reason is revelatory. Although specialists may have some acquaintance with other subject matters, only regarding their own are they familiar with a broad spectrum of faculty members, programs, and scholarly activities. Therefore, unless one candidate is clearly superior to all others (a rare situation), each professor will find "the best" to be the best in that specialist's field and try to forge a majority in favor of that candidate. As the infighting continues, the field most likely to be neglected is the one currently unrepresented; it is least known by the members yet most in need of an appointment. In the end, however, whichever professor is politically savvy and most determined carries the day. If, after a year or two, another opening appears and again the same area is disregarded, the department will become lopsided, perhaps for decades.

Why did this situation develop? Because the dean allowed the department to advertise the position as open. What should have happened is that when the department suggested that compromise, the dean should have responded, "Most of the nineteenth century is uncovered. Unless that's the specialty you announce, the search is over". The department would be upset but would likely bow to the dean in order to make an appointment.

Eventually, if the dean monitors the search process carefully, the department will settle on a candidate who focuses on the romantic era. As a result, the students will benefit and have the opportunity to study the music of Mendelssohn, Chopin, and Verdi, among so many other favorites. Even the faculty may eventually appreciate the perspective of their new colleague and realize the wisdom of offering broader coverage.

In any case, discord is likely to accompany the process. Indeed, if for nefarious reasons someone wanted to create turmoil in an amiable department, I cannot think of a more effective strategy than offering the members an opportunity to undertake a search. Even if they do not reach consensus, the members should consider themselves fortunate if their good relations survive.

# Chapter 15

## *The Ambiguities of Affirmative Action*

When departments undertake faculty searches, one issue almost sure to arise is the role affirmative action should play in the decision. The matter is far more complicated than usually assumed, and my major aim here is to show why.

First, the term "affirmative action" refers to two entirely different policies. One is taking appropriate steps to eradicate practices of racial, gender, religious, or ethnic discrimination. Such *procedural affirmative action*, as I call it, is intended to guarantee that applicants for positions are judged on their merits, not their identities. Steps to ensure procedural affirmative action include open announcements of opportunities, blind reviewing, and a variety of efforts to eliminate from decision procedures any policies that harbor prejudice, however vestigial.

In another sense of "affirmative action", which I call *preferential affirmative action*, the term signifies making special efforts to recruit individuals who meet institutional goals related, for example, to racial, gender, or ethnic identity. Doing so calls for attending to the same criteria that procedural affirmative action deems irrelevant. Whereas procedural affirmative action is uncontroversial, preferential affirmative action is not, and in the remainder of this discussion, my use of the term "affirmative action" should be understood as referring to "preferential affirmative action".

What is the point of affirmative action? Is it to offset past discrimination, counteract present unfairness, or achieve future equality? The first is often referred to as "compensation", the second as "a level playing field", and the third as "diversity".

Note that each of these aims can be defended independently of the others. Compensation for past wrongs may be owed, although at present the playing field is level and future diversity is not sought. Or the playing field at present may not be level, although compensation for past wrongs is not owed and future diversity is not sought. Or future diversity may be sought, although compensation for past wrongs is not owed and at present the playing field is level.

Of course, all three factors might be relevant, but each requires a different justification and calls for a different remedy. For example, past wrongs would be offset if suitable compensation were made, but once provided to the appropriate recipients, no other steps would be needed. Present wrongs would be corrected if actions were taken that would level the playing field, but doing so would be consistent with unequal outcomes. Future equality would require continuing attention to ensure that an appropriate balance, once achieved, would never be lost. Thus defenders of affirmative action would favor at least one of these policies but not necessarily more than one.

Regarding the frequently cited appeal to diversity, the concept itself, if unmodified, is vacuous. Consider, for example, a sample of the innumerable respects in which people can differ: age, religion, nationality, regional background, economic resources, military experience, bodily appearance, physical soundness, sexual orientation, marital status, ethical standards, political commitments, or cultural values. The crucial question is: Which sorts of diversity should be sought?

Imagine a 10-person philosophy department that has no African American, no woman, no non-American, no person under 50, no non-Christian, no registered Republican, none whose doctoral degree is from other than an Ivy League university, none who served in a war, none who is homosexual, none who was ever on welfare, none who is physically challenged, none whose work is outside the analytic tradition, none who specializes in aesthetics, and none who is widely heralded for success as a teacher. When the next appointment is made, which characteristics should be stressed so as to render this department more diverse? I know of no compelling answer.

To put the matter vividly, suppose that the 10 finalists for a position in that department include an African American, a woman, an Argentinian, a 30-year-old, a Buddhist, a Republican, someone whose doctoral degree is from Indiana University, a veteran, someone who was once on welfare, someone who uses a wheelchair, a homosexual, a specialist in continental philosophy, an aesthetician, and a widely acclaimed teacher. Which one should be favored purely on grounds of enhancing diversity? The question is unanswerable.

Suppose the suggestion is made that the sorts of diversity to be sought are those of groups that have suffered discrimination. The problem with this approach is clearly put by John Kekes:

> It is true that American blacks, Native Americans, Hispanics, and women have suffered injustices as a group. But so have homosexuals, epileptics, the urban and the rural poor, the physically ugly, those whose careers were ruined by McCarthyism, prostitutes, the obese, and so forth….
>
> There have been some attempts to deny that there is an analogy between these two classes of victims. It has been said that the first were unjustly discriminated against due to racial or sexual prejudice and that this is not true of the second. This is indeed so. But should we accept the suggestion…that the only form of injustice relevant to preferential treatment is that which is due to racial or sexual prejudice? Injustice occurs in many forms, and those who value justice will surely object to all of them.[1]

Kekes's reasoning is cogent. In addition, another difficulty looms for the proposal to seek diversity only of groups that have suffered discrimination. Consider, for instance, a department in which most of the faculty members are women. In certain fields, for example, nursing, dental hygiene, and elementary education, such departments are common. If diversity by gender is of value, then such a department, when making its next appointment, should prefer a man. Yet men as a group have not been victims of discrimination. On the other hand, Jews and Asians have been victims of discrimination but do not at present suffer from minimal representation. Thus the question of which groups need enhancement to achieve diversity cannot be answered satisfactorily by an appeal to history.

Nor is the situation clarified by arguing that the appeal to diversity favors those from a group who experience the world from a distinctive standpoint. Celia Wolf-Devine has aptly described this claim as a form of "stereotyping" that is "demeaning". As she puts it, "A Hispanic who is a Republican is no less a Hispanic, and a woman who is not a feminist is no less a woman".[2] Furthermore, are Hispanic men and women supposed to have the same point of view in virtue of their common ethnicity, or are they supposed to have different points of view in virtue of their different genders? And why suppose that a person's point of view is determined only by race, gender, or ethnicity? Why not also by the numerous other significant respects in which people differ, such as age, religion, sexual orientation, political outlook, and so on?

Every affirmative action plan calls for giving preference to members of certain groups, but the concept of preference itself is unclear. For example, imagine a search for an assistant professor in which 100 persons apply, and among them are some who are members of a group designated for affirmative action. Let us refer to those individuals as AA candidates.

Suppose the dean has permitted five applicants to be invited for campus interviews. After studying all the vitae and sets of recommendations, the department ranks 10 candidates as outstanding, 20 as good, 50 as merely qualified, and 20 as unqualified. Let us suppose that four applicants are AA candidates, and among them one is ranked as outstanding, one as good, one as merely qualified, and one as unqualified.

The key question is: Assuming AA candidates are to be preferred, what forms of preference are called for? One possibility is to agree to interview any AA candidate who is outstanding, regardless of the merits of any other outstanding candidates. Another possibility is to agree to interview any AA candidate who is good, even though many other candidates are stronger. Yet another possibility is to agree to interview any AA candidate who is qualified, even though again most candidates are stronger. A theoretical possibility is to interview even unqualified AA candidates, although I know of no one who would support that policy, so let us set it aside. What remains are three different models of preference, any of which might be defended.

Next, assume that two AA candidates are chosen for interviews, one who was ranked as outstanding and another ranked as good. Afterwards, the department places the outstanding candidate second and the other tenth. Does giving preference to AA candidates require that the second candidate be offered the position? And if the candidate ranked second receives a more attractive offer and withdraws from consideration, need the candidate now ranked tenth be preferred?

Of course, an AA candidate may be ranked the highest, thus avoiding any problems. Otherwise, the call for giving preference requires an interpretation that is rarely, if ever, announced beforehand.

Furthermore, even assuming that the department has explicitly agreed to a policy regarding preference, the question remains whether that policy will be made public. Suppose, for instance, that the administration has told the department that its next appointment needs to be an AA candidate. Shouldn't that information be publicized, so that those who are members of the groups in question and those who are not can plan accordingly? Surely, those who have instituted a policy of preference believe that their action is within moral and legal bounds. Therefore no one should object to stating that policy without equivocation. Yet the usual approach is to keep such information under wraps.

Such secrecy, however, leads to difficulties. For instance, during my years as an administrator I once met with a candidate who was considering our school's offer of a faculty position and sought my assurance that he would have been chosen regardless of affirmative action. I responded truthfully that he was held in high regard but that I didn't know the answer to his concern. Yet I believe he was entitled to raise the matter. For whatever the steps required by a school's affirmative action policy, surely they should not be hidden.

In addition, circumstances matter. Consider a department that has never appointed a woman and, when given a promising opportunity, refuses even to interview one. Suppose the dean insists that in the next search process some women should be interviewed, and if a woman with a superlative record is found, she should be appointed. Would opponents of affirmative action object? I think not.

On the other hand, consider a department with 40% women that announces its intention to achieve a goal of 50% women, and in its next search prefers a minimally qualified woman to a man who is widely regarded as far more promising as a researcher, teacher, and contributor to the life of the department. If the dean insists that the man be appointed, would proponents of affirmative action be upset? Again, I think not.

Both of these cases are admittedly extreme, though not entirely unrealistic, but the lesson is that presuming affirmative action to be at odds with merit, as its opponents do, or to be a means of obtaining justice, as its defenders do, is an oversimplification. The context matters.

To sum up, when the issue of affirmative action arises, faculty members should clarify whether procedural or preferential affirmative action is under discussion; whether the goal is compensation, a level playing field, or diversity; what sorts of diversity are sought; what sorts of preference are proposed; whether the policy will be made public; and whether any special circumstances are part of the context. Without this information, any discussion of affirmative action is likely to generate more heat than light.

## Notes

1  John Kekes, "The Injustice of Strong Affirmative Action," in Steven M. Cahn, ed., *Affirmative Action and the University: A Philosophical Inquiry* (Philadelphia: Temple University Press, 1993), 151.
2  Celia Wolf-Devine, "Proportional Representation of Women and Minorities," in Cahn, 230.

# Chapter 16

# *Departmental Voting*

As a search process continues, the time comes for choosing candidates for interviews. At this point departments are prone to make an error in their voting procedure that leads to unfortunate results.

To see how, consider a department that plans to choose eight candidates to be interviewed for one opening. At the meeting where the voting is to occur, the suggestion is made that each member of the 10-person department be given four votes and the eight candidates receiving the most votes be invited.

The idea may at first glance appear reasonable but it is not. For suppose that nine of the 10 members prefer candidate A to all others, then candidate B, then C, then D, and on down to candidate Z. One member of the department, however, prefers the candidates in reverse order, rating candidate Z the highest, Y the next highest, X next, and so on down to candidate A, who is rated the lowest.

Now the voting takes place. Nine members vote for candidates A, B, C, and D. The other member votes for

Z, Y, X, and W. So A, B, C, D, Z, Y, X, and W are the only candidates to receive votes and hence are invited for interviews.

The problem, of course, is that almost every member of the department hasn't the slightest interest in Z, Y, X, or W, preferring E, F, G, H, and every other candidate to Z, Y, X, and W. Yet Z, Y, X, and W have been invited. What has gone wrong?

The procedure has violated an essential principle of fair voting. Each voter should have been given the same number of votes as the number of candidates to be selected. Thus in this case each member should have been given eight votes, because eight applicants were to be chosen. Using that principle would have resulted in invitations to A, B, C, D, E, F, G, and H, who were preferred by the vast majority of the department. Z, Y, X, and W were the candidates least preferred by almost all department members and should not have been invited.

In short, voting may proceed in a variety of ways, but in any case each voter should be allowed to express as many preferences as the number of people to be selected. Departmental decisions of this sort can be bitter enough without adding to the mix an irrational decision procedure.

# Chapter 17

## *Interviewing Candidates*

After voting takes place, initial interviews are scheduled. These typically take place at a professional conference or by Skype. Usually several faculty members will talk individually for 30 to 40 minutes with a dozen or so candidates.

Those being interviewed can perform well or poorly, but so can those conducting the interviews. Much has been written about how to be interviewed,[1] but I want to concentrate on the infrequently discussed matter of how to conduct an academic interview. Here are some suggestions:

1.  Ask all applicants the same basic questions, set in advance. Follow-ups will differ in each case, but if all interviews are structured alike, a source of unfairness is minimized. Suppose, for instance, that candidate A is preferred over candidate B, and one reason is that B offered a weak answer to a particular question. If A was not asked the same question, why presume A's answer would have been better than B's? Perhaps the question itself was problematic.

2. Keep notes of what was said. As the hours wear on, attention wanders and one candidate begins to blur into another. Weeks later, when the candidates are evaluated at a department meeting or in discussion with a dean, the written record will prove invaluable.

3. Ask one question at a time, thereby avoiding this sort of pileup: "Why did you choose to write about Plato's theory of Forms? What is the theory? And, by the way, what do you think of Aristotle's criticisms of the theory?"

4. The best questions are short. If a question requires a long setup, it's probably not an effective question.

5. Interviewers may be tempted to engage in an extended discussion of a comment made by the candidate but that temptation should be resisted. Time is limited, and the purpose of an interview is not to offer departmental colleagues the opportunity to display their erudition or analytic skills. One rule of thumb: Interviewers should talk much less than the candidate.

6. Inquiring about a candidate's dissertation is sensible, but concentrating on it almost exclusively is limiting. How about asking: "Tell us something about your areas of interest outside your thesis". Or even: "Do you have intellectual pursuits beyond our field?" After all, a candidate is being considered for an appointment not only to a department but to an entire faculty. As such, the individual may be called on to participate in multidisciplinary programs, offer lectures on broad themes, or share in decisions affecting the departmental or college

curricula. Some attention, therefore, should be paid to the range of a candidate's intellectual horizon.

7. Candidates are expected to be effective teachers; thus some pedagogical questions should be asked. For example, "What materials would you cover in an introductory course? Or "What do you think of the practice of grading students?"

8. Candidates are also expected to assume a fair share of the day-to-day tasks that are an inescapable part of academic life. Hence a revealing question might be: "Would you be willing to serve on the library committee, assessing our holdings and recommending works to be acquired?" If one candidate replies, "I would rather spend time on my research", and another says, "I'd be happy to help in any way I can", you have learned what you need to know.

9. Do not ask personal questions that have no bearing on performance as a faculty member. For example, no one should inquire, "Do you think you might be too old for this position?" Or "Will your spouse be living with you?" If a colleague poses such an inappropriate query, other interviewers should intervene and return the discussion to suitable topics.

10. Always be polite. Never engage in insults, laugh derisively at an answer, act in a condescending manner, or display a lack of interest in the proceedings. Remember that you, too, were once an applicant.

In sum, interviewers should make every effort to be kind and fair. They should not, however, be credulous.

Challenging questions should be asked and cogent answers expected. Those candidates who do not provide them should be eliminated from consideration, not out of animosity but from a commitment to appointing colleagues who give evidence of excelling as scholars, teachers, and contributors to the academic community.

## Note

1   See, for instance, *From Student to Scholar*, 25–32.

# Chapter 18

## *Tenure and Academic Freedom*

Eventually a department is called on to decide whether an individual to whom it offered a term appointment should be granted a tenured position. While members may disagree about this decision, any dispute takes place from a standpoint shared by virtually all: belief in the tenure system itself, according to which those who possess tenure hold lifetime appointments, revocable only in rare instances of gross incompetence or moral turpitude. Yet reference to this prerogative invariably gives rise to the same questions: Why should anyone receive permanent job security? And doesn't tenure pamper the indolent and protect the incompetent?

Academic tenure is not as singular as often supposed. In most organizations of university size, employees, whether at lower ranks or in middle management, are rarely dismissed for cause. As a result of poor performance they may be passed over for promotion, given lateral transfers, or occasionally demoted but are rarely ever discharged. While plant closings or fiscal crises may precipitate worker layoffs, tenured professors, too, face the loss of their positions if a department is phased out or a school closes.

Even the mechanics of the tenure system are hardly unique. Consider large law firms, which routinely recruit new associates with the understanding that after several years they will either be offered some variety of permanent position or required to depart. Colleges make similar arrangements with beginning faculty members.

Despite such analogies, however, tenure undoubtedly provides professors an unusual degree of latitude and security. They are privileged to explore any area of interest and to proceed in whatever manner they wish. No one may dictate to them that certain subjects are taboo, that certain methods of inquiry are illegitimate, or that certain conclusions are unacceptable.

Tenure thus guarantees academic freedom, the right of all qualified persons to discover, teach, and publish the truth as they see it within their fields of competence. Where academic freedom is secure, students enter classrooms with the assurance that instructors are espousing their own beliefs, not mouthing some orthodoxy they have been programmed to repeat. Likewise, academic freedom guarantees that no ideological test is imposed to determine who will be appointed to the faculty. Competence, not creed, is the criterion.

Although academic freedom is widely seen as valuable, it is threatened whenever anyone seeks to stifle free inquiry in the name of some cause that supposedly demands everyone's unthinking allegiance. Some, for example, have sought to have a department adopt an official stance on issues unrelated to its educational mission. Free inquiry, however, is impeded when certain opinions are officially declared false and others true. Schools are not established to inform the public where a majority of the faculty stands on any issue, whether mathematical, scientific, or political. Whether an argument for the existence of God is sound or our government's foreign policy misguided are matters for discussion, not decree.

Maintaining free inquiry requires that all points of view be entitled to a hearing. Unfortunately, some whether from inside or outside academia have attempted to interfere with a campus speaker's presentation on the grounds that they find the views expressed to be unpalatable. So long as the lecturer remains civil, however, no one at the school, whether professors, students, or administrators, should block any individual from expressing ideas. No matter how noxious they may be, the greater danger lies in stifling them, for when one person's opinion is silenced, no one else's may be uttered in safety.

But might academic freedom be preserved without tenure, perhaps by some form of multi-year contracts? The problem besetting any alternative scheme is that it could too easily be misused, opening faculty members to attack because of their opinions.

A key feature of the tenure system is that those who hold tenure decide whether it should be granted to others. Thus those who judge are not facing a conflict of interest, because their own tenure is not at stake. In any system of multi-year contracts, however, the question arises: Who should decide whether a contract ought to be renewed? If the decision is placed in the hands of other tenured professors, they would be voting while realizing that their own contracts would eventually be up for renewal. The result would be a conflict of interest. After all, if I support your renewal, will you support or oppose mine? Worse, the decision might be made by administrators with an ax to grind, favoring contract renewal for professors who have supported administrative initiatives. Such a system would produce an atmosphere of suspicion and recrimination, antithetical to independent thinking.

Unquestionably, the tenure system has dangers, but none as great as those that would attend its abandonment. To adapt a remark about democracy offered by Winston Churchill, tenure may be the worst system ever devised, except for all the others.

To defend the tenure system in principle, however, is not to applaud the ways it has been implemented. Without doubt many departments have supported candidates for tenure too liberally. Instead of individuals being required to demonstrate why they deserve tenure, a department has been expected to demonstrate why they don't. In court a person ought to be presumed not guilty until the evidence shows otherwise, but in matters of special skill you ought not be supposed excellent until so proven. A school's failure to observe this guideline results in a faculty encumbered with deadwood, and more than a few departments suffer from this unfortunate phenomenon.

Yet decisions whether to grant tenure can present difficult problems and have been known to cause hostilities that last for decades. We have seen how the appointment process can lead to a conflict, but it may be a mere skirmish compared with the campus war that can break out over a tenure decision. Yet unpleasant as events may become, faculty members need to act conscientiously because the future of their departments may be at stake. Even a single ill-advised decision may lead to years of disruption, bringing tenure itself into disrepute and thereby threatening that academic freedom the system is intended to preserve. In short, wise choices are a blessing, foolish ones a blight.

# Part IV
# Finale

# Chapter 19

## *Expressing Gratitude*

One noticeable feature of academic life is how much time is spent arguing against the views of others. After all, for a paper to be thought worthy of presentation or an article to be considered publishable, it needs to express dissatisfaction to some extent with prevailing opinion.

Indeed, criticism is the lifeblood of academia. If you can't deal with negative assessments, you are akin to a trial attorney who can't handle disagreements or a specialist in emergency medicine who can't deal with crises. You've chosen the wrong profession.

Such a focus on finding fault leads easily to a lack of sympathy for the efforts of others. For instance, years ago I attended a departmental colloquium where the speaker offered a talk that I found clear, insightful, and compelling. When the time came for comments, I expressed appreciation for her fine presentation. The audience waited for my criticisms, but I had none. I merely wanted to offer a compliment. My attitude, however, appeared to shock my colleagues. Wasn't I going to try to demonstrate a mistake in her argument? Wasn't I going to suggest the limitations of her approach? Wasn't I going to call attention to a reference she had omitted? If not, why had I spoken?

Similarly, I recall that soon after the publication of the late Robert Nozick's remarkable book *Philosophical Explanations* I saw him at a national meeting of the American Philosophical Association, where I told him how much I admired his new work.[1] Then, however, I apologized for repeating what he had surely heard many times before. To my surprise, he replied ruefully that, in fact, I was the first person there to have complimented him. Others had sought him out but only to express disagreements; no word of encouragement had passed their lips.

Not offering appreciation when merited indicates a lack of manners, a failure to treat others appropriately. The link between manners and ethics was noted by Hobbes, who referred to manners as small morals,[2] an insight John Dewey expressed more alliteratively by stating that "manners are but minor morals".[3]

Academics may be prone to overlook the connection because too many are led in graduate school to view scholarly inquiry as a competition in which you score points by refuting others, rather than a cooperative enterprise in which participants reason together to enhance understanding. Indeed, when colleagues seek to move the process forward, they deserve thanks.

Appreciation should also extend to students. However unsophisticated their remarks may be, so long as they are trying to make a contribution to the discussion, they deserve respect. Again, doctoral education fails to instill the appropriate attitude.

Neither rudeness nor arrogance belongs in a classroom. Instead of an instructor's reacting to a student's opinion by declaring, "You've missing an obvious point", a more appropriate reply would be: "You may be on to something, but let's consider a possible objection to your view".

Similarly, when comments are offered at a professional lecture, they should begin on a positive note, even if only to thank the speaker for raising provocative issues. Such politeness will not diminish the significance of any challenge offered but will reinforce the principle that criticism is consistent with courtesy.

The travails of academic life would be lessened if professors emphasized not only the importance of correctness but also a concern for kindness.

## Notes

1  Robert Nozick, *Philosophical Explanations* (Cambridge, MA: Harvard University Press, 1981).
2  Thomas Hobbes, *Leviathan* (Cleveland and New York: The World Publishing Company, 1963), 122.
3  John Dewey, *Democracy and Education: The Middle Works of John Dewey, 1899–1924*, ed. Jo Ann Boydston (Carbondale, IL: Southern Illinois University Press, 1980), 9:22.

# Chapter 20

## *My Early Years in Academia*

In reflecting on life in academia, I find myself returning to events that occurred in the first decade of my career. Undoubtedly, they contributed much to my outlook; hence I think it fitting to conclude these essays with a brief account of the people and places of my younger days.

## 1

In 1959, after graduating from Woodmere Academy (now Lawrence Woodmere Academy), where most memorably I studied Latin for a year with the celebrated poet and translator Rolfe Humphries, I entered Columbia College. I registered as pre-law but still lacked a career goal. Two years later, as yet unsure of my vocation and seeking further understanding of the legal profession, I enrolled in a course titled "Philosophy of Law". I did not realize that the professor, Ernest Nagel, was an internationally renowned philosopher of science, but I became enamored of his brilliance, erudition, and modest demeanor. He spoke so clearly and answered questions so patiently that

I was inspired to try to emulate him. Thus I began to consider pursuing the study of philosophy. While taking a second course of his devoted to epistemology, I ventured into his office and inquired whether he thought I might become a philosopher. His response was encouraging and consequently my tentative plan to attend law school was shelved.

## 2

Wishing to stay in New York, I applied to and was accepted at Columbia's Graduate Department of Philosophy. I soon realized, however, that I needed a specialty and was not sure which to select. I did not have sufficient background in science to choose Professor Nagel's area. I had an interest in history, particularly American history, but no special concern for the philosophy of history. I had performed extensively as a pianist and organist but preferred playing music to discussing it. I had knowledge of Judaism, but the philosophy department offered no courses in philosophy of religion.

Hence when I went to register for the first time, I chose haphazardly, selecting a class in American philosophy and another in the religion department. Then I asked the advisor if he had any suggestions. He recommended "Philosophical Analysis", a course to be taught by Professor Richard Taylor, who had just arrived from Brown University. I knew nothing about him and had no idea what was meant by "philosophical analysis", but lacking promising alternatives, I enrolled. Little did I know that my life was about to change.

Professor Taylor's teaching style, which he called "the blackboard and chalk method", was a revelation. The approach didn't require mastery of either the history of philosophy or current journal literature. Rather, he wrote on the board the steps of an argument, and students were supposed to decide if the reasoning was sound.

The task appeared straightforward, yet offering an answer that could withstand criticism proved difficult. Nevertheless, I welcomed this challenge as it depended not on extensive research but only on hard thinking.

The first topic for discussion was an argument for fatalism. I didn't realize it was Professor Taylor's own, and I submitted a paper defending it against criticisms he had suggested we consider. When a couple of days later he returned my essay, I was stunned by his laudatory comments. Indeed, he urged me to prepare the piece for publication and use it as a chapter of my dissertation. Suddenly my life had focus: I knew my specialty, my advisor, and my calling.

From then on, I attended every graduate class Professor Taylor taught and was a regular visitor to his office. Eventually, as he had predicted, the paper was published and served as a chapter of my dissertation.[1] But as I finished writing my thesis, Professor Taylor left Columbia to join the faculty at the University of Rochester, and under the generous sponsorship of Professor Arthur Danto, I completed my work.

Nevertheless, I stayed in touch with Professor Taylor, who kindly returned to New York to attend my dissertation defense. Indeed, for a few summers, I visited him at his home in Trumansburg, just north of Ithaca. There he kept his beehives, for, as I discovered, he was world renowned as an apiarist and wrote a column for the leading beekeeping journal. In fact, as he told me, he was better known among beekeepers than among philosophers.

## 3

The time had now come for me to seek a faculty position. Appointments then were far easier to obtain than they became a few years later, and one fall morning the secretary in the Philosophy Department asked if I would like to be interviewed for a position the next year at Vassar College. I hesitated because I had not anticipated a post at a women's college (only later did Vassar become coed), but fortunately the secretary scheduled an interview, conducted by the longtime chair of the Vassar department, Vernon Venable. In those days, openings were not publicly announced, and Professor Venable's search procedure consisted of visiting potential candidates only at Harvard, Yale, and Columbia.

During our brief meeting, he asked whether I was a Wittgensteinian. Though not entirely sure of his meaning, I replied that I wasn't. That answer turned out to be helpful because, as Professor Venable subsequently explained, he didn't care for the work of Wittgenstein. Afterwards he asked me to examine the Vassar catalogue and indicate which philosophy courses I would prefer to teach, which I would be willing to teach, and which I would not want to teach.

That task was not difficult until I came to a course titled "Philosophy of Education". I had not heard of this subject and wondered into which category I should place it. I reasoned fallaciously that because I was interested in philosophy and in education (having taught religious studies to grade school students), I would also be interested in philosophy of education. Therefore I listed it among the subjects I would prefer to teach.

Little did I realize that expressing enthusiasm for that course would be a primary reason I would be chosen for the position. In fact, the department was required to offer the course every semester to meet the needs of the education students, and no member of the philosophy faculty or any applicants wanted to teach it. Ironically, the field became a specialty of mine, and soon after leaving Vassar, having taught the course four times, I edited my own anthology, which in a second edition remains in use.[2]

Before I began at Vassar, though, I had a free term, and Professor Taylor recommended me to the faculty at Dartmouth College, where someone was needed for one semester to teach discussion sections of their introductory course. I gratefully accepted an offer and spent a delightful term in Hanover, New Hampshire, where I heard captivating lectures to the entire class by professors Willis Doney, Timothy Duggan, and Bernard Gert. All three welcomed me, and as a beginner I was grateful for their cordiality.

The department sponsored colloquia, and I still remember the visit by the eminent historian of philosophy, Father Frederick Copleston. After his talk, he spent the rest of the evening answering with remarkable ease complex questions posed by faculty members seeking his assistance in handling especially challenging interpretative problems in the history of philosophy. Copleston's mastery was astounding.

# 4

When fall came, I arrived at Vassar, and the two years I spent there proved to be among the happiest of my academic career. The students were first-rate and enthusiastic, while the faculty was knowledgeable and collegial. Indeed, I developed a special relationship with three members of the department.

One was John O'Connor, who later became executive director of the American Philosophical Association. John had earned his Ph.D. at Harvard, while serving as a teaching assistant for both Quine and Rawls. John was an amazingly sharp thinker yet easy to talk to. I learned much from our many conversations and enjoyed evenings in his company.

Another valued colleague was Garrett Vander Veer, who earned his degree at Yale, where he had been a student of the eminent idealist philosopher Brand Blanshard. While Garry and I had different philosophical backgrounds, I admired his academic integrity, the unwillingness to compromise reasonable standards. He was also a superb tennis player and skilled golfer, an unusual combination.

A third philosopher of note was Frank Tillman, whom I had met when we both attended the philosophical discussion group that convened at Richard Taylor's apartment during his years at Columbia. After I had been at Vassar for a few weeks, Frank invited me to his large office. There he showed me piles of materials that he hoped to shape into a reader in aesthetics to be published by Harper & Row, for whom he worked as a consultant. He asked if I might help him complete the volume and become its co-editor. I had no experience with such work but was pleased to participate. Eventually the book became my first anthology, introducing me to the world of college publishing and resulting in my lifelong interest in such projects.[3]

## 5

Although I enjoyed the ambiance at Vassar, I had always hoped to return to New York City; hence I was delighted when I received an invitation from Sidney Hook to join the faculty at New York University's Washington Square College in Greenwich Village.

The next five years, 1968–1973, were a time of disruption to our country and NYU, but for me they were a period of growth and excitement. I taught large undergraduate courses, sometimes with as many as a hundred or more students, took on graduate seminars with talented future scholars, some of whom would become nationally known, and accepted departmental and college-wide administrative assignments. Chief among these was serving as head of the school's Educational Policy Committee, which was responsible for approving every department's proposed curricular changes. My responsibilities led me to meet many of the College's leading faculty members, an opportunity I relished.

Within the department, I welcomed working with Professor Hook, whose writings I greatly admired. While he was a fierce debater concerning the issues of the day, he was always generous to students and colleagues. Although the mailboxes of the other members of the department were virtually empty, his was invariably stuffed with correspondence from around the world. Yet his celebrity mattered no more to him than teaching a class or providing a letter of recommendation. I remain grateful for his many kindnesses.

Almost every day I ate lunch with my colleague James Rachels. In New York City, most faculty members do not spend much time at school but treat the entire city as a campus. Jim and I, however, were regularly in our offices, and, as we were about the same age and at the same stage of our careers, we conversed endlessly about philosophy and academic life. He was remarkably affable, easygoing, and straightforward. The trait most foreign to him was pomposity. Typical was his reply to someone who asked about "films he had attended": "I don't attend films, " he replied. "I go to movies".

Unfortunately, after we had been at NYU for a couple of years, the school suffered a financial crisis and the administrators, seeking to reduce the size of the faculty, urged that any untenured faculty members who were able to leave, should do so. Jim decided to accept an offer from the University of Miami, and when he departed, I was willing to consider other possibilities.

## 6

An unusual one appeared at the University of Vermont, which advertised for a departmental chair. When the head of their search committee, renowned psychologist George Albee, unexpectedly came to New York to visit me, I learned of a strange situation. Until several years before, few philosophers had been appointed, and they were part of a single philosophy and religion department. When the university rapidly increased in size, the number of philosophers did as well. Unfortunately, the process was handled without regard for appropriate academic procedures. The result was a large but undistinguished group of faculty, which considered itself estranged from the contemporary philosophical scene. They were soon at loggerheads with the administration, and Professor Albee was asked to head an ad hoc committee to find someone who could lead the building of a first-class, independent philosophy department. He wondered if I might be willing to accept the assignment.

Had the situation at NYU been settled, I am sure I would have turned him down. But the challenge was appealing, and with some naïveté I decided to pursue the opportunity. When eventually a formal offer was made, I accepted.

The task, however, proved far more difficult than I had imagined. The dean had invited me without the support of most of the faculty. They had opposed every outside candidate and, with a couple of exceptions, resisted evaluation by usual academic standards. The only positive feature of the situation was that most of the department's faculty were untenured and subject to annual reappointment. After speaking with each of them at length and assessing their records, I recommended that four not be asked to return.

The matter became a cause célèbre. Yet after several months of turmoil the administration backed my recommendation. Three of the four were not reappointed, and the fourth was warned that unless he soon obtained his long-sought doctoral degree, he would not be continued; the following year he voluntarily departed.

Thus the department needed at least three new faculty members, and I had the primary responsibility for choosing them. The advertisement I placed resulted in the receipt of more than 700 applications. I studied each, then at the American Philosophical Association's Eastern Division meeting I conducted interviews by myself and invited the most promising candidates to campus.

Eventually, after persuading the dean to allow four appointments, I chose Patricia Kitcher, Philip Kitcher, William Mann, and George Sher. I doubt if ever in my career I made a wiser decision. While their philosophical interests varied widely, all were outstanding teachers and future leading researchers who would eventually hold chairs in philosophy. At the time I met them, though, their total publication record consisted of a single essay. (Since then, they have written more than 25 books and 300 articles.)

Each, however, was enormously conscientious and committed to work tirelessly to enhance the department, locally and nationally. The task was arduous, but our effort succeeded, and the University of Vermont gained a reputation for excellence in philosophy that remains to this day. Indeed, any list of the strongest undergraduate philosophy departments in the United States invariably includes the University of Vermont.

We conducted searches with the utmost care, and our appointments were so strong that over time at least eight members of the department went on to professorships in leading doctoral programs. Given that for nearly a half century thousands of undergraduates at the University of Vermont have had the opportunity to study philosophy with the guidance of an outstanding faculty, I consider the building of that department, however onerous, to have been a major accomplishment.

# 7

Subsequently I entered the world of foundations, where during a five-year period I worked at the Exxon Education Foundation, the Rockefeller Foundation, and the National Endowment for the Humanities. Then I became an administrator at the City University of New York Graduate Center, where I served for nearly a decade as Dean of Graduate Studies, then Provost and Vice President for Academic Affairs, then Acting President. Eventually I returned full-time to the Philosophy Program and for over 25 years taught and advised numerous doctoral students while continuing to write and edit books.[4]

These later years were indeed satisfying, due most importantly to the many dedicated students with whom I was privileged to work. While most of them have disappeared from my view, quite a number have stayed in touch, and several have collaborated with me on book projects. All have done more than they know to enrich my professional life.

Yet as my brother, Victor L. Cahn, once wrote, "Memories from youth tend to be indelible. Happy or sad, they shape and color our lives".[5] Such has been the case for me. And on that note I bring these reflections to a close.

## Notes

1   The paper, "Fatalistic Arguments," originally appeared in *The Journal of Philosophy* 61, no. 10 (1964), 295–305, was incorporated in my first book *Fate, Logic, and Time* (New Haven: Yale University Press, 1967, reprinted by Wipf and Stock Publishers, 2002), and was included in Steven M. Cahn and Maureen Eckert, eds., *Fate, Time, and Language: An Essay on Free Will by David Foster Wallace* (New York: Columbia University Press, 2011), 93–106.

2   Steven M. Cahn, *Classic and Contemporary Readings in the Philosophy of Education*, Second Edition (New York: Oxford University Press, 2012).

3   Frank A. Tillman and Steven M. Cahn, eds., *Philosophy of Art and Aesthetics: From Plato to Wittgenstein* (New York: Harper & Row, 1969).

4   A detailed account of this later period is found in Steven M. Cahn, *The Road Traveled and Other Essays* (Eugene, OR: Wipf and Stock Publishers, 2019), 91–100.

5   See *Classic and Contemporary Readings in the Philosophy of Education*, x.

# Sources

1. APA blog (May 14, 2018). Reprinted with permission.
2. APA blog (March 8, 2019). Reprinted with permission.
3. APA blog (November 14, 2017). Reprinted with permission.
4. *Teaching Philosophy*, 27, 4, 2004. Reprinted with permission of the journal.
5. APA blog (June 8, 2019). Reprinted with permission
6. APA blog (November 28, 2019). Reprinted with permission.
7. APA blog (December 26, 2019). Reprinted with permission.
8. APA blog (May 11, 2017). Reprinted with permission.
9. *Newsletter on Teaching Philosophy*, 18, 2, 2019. Reprinted by permission of the American Philosophical Association.
10. *Teaching Philosophy: A Guide*, Routledge, 2018, 32–36. Reprinted by permission of the publisher.
11. APA blog (August 28, 2019). Reprinted with permission.
12. *Saints and Scamps: Ethics in Academia*, 25th Anniversary Edition, Rowman & Littlefield, 2011, 34–39. Reprinted by permission of the publisher.
13. *Inside Academia: Professors, Politics, and Policies*, Rutgers University Press, 2019, 73–75. Reprinted with permission of the publisher.
14. APA blog (January 22, 2018). Reprinted with permission
15. APA blog (February 28, 2018). Reprinted with permission.
16. APA blog (January 17, 2017). Reprinted with permission.
17. APA blog (October 24, 2019). Reprinted with permission.
18. *Inside Academia: Professors, Politics, and Policies*. 81–84. Reprinted with permission of the publisher.
19. APA blog (April 11, 2019). Reprinted with permission.
20. *The Road Traveled and Other Essays*. Wipf and Stock Publishers, 2019, 83–91. Reprinted with permission of the publisher.

# Works by Steven M. Cahn

## Books Authored

*Fate, Logic, and Time*
    Yale University Press, 1967
    Ridgeview Publishing Company, 1982
    Wipf and Stock Publishers, 2004
*A New Introduction to Philosophy*
    Harper & Row, 1971
    University Press of America, 1986
    Wipf and Stock Publishers, 2004
*The Eclipse of Excellence: A Critique of American Higher Education*
    (Foreword by Charles Frankel)
    Public Affairs Press, 1973
    Wipf and Stock Publishers, 2004
*Education and the Democratic Ideal*
    Nelson-Hall Company, 1979
    Wipf and Stock Publishers, 2004
*Saints and Scamps: Ethics in Academia*
    Rowman & Littlefield, 1986
    Revised Edition, 1994
    25th Anniversary Edition, 2011
    (Foreword by Thomas H. Powell)
*Philosophical Explorations: Freedom, God, and Goodness*
    Prometheus Books, 1989
*Puzzles & Perplexities: Collected Essays*
    Rowman & Littlefield, 2002
    Second Edition, Lexington Books, 2007
*God, Reason, and Religion*
    Thomson/Wadsworth, 2006
*From Student to Scholar: A Candid Guide to Becoming a Professor*
    (Foreword by Catharine R. Stimpson)
    Columbia University Press, 2008

*Polishing Your Prose: How to Turn First Drafts into Finished Work*
  (with Victor L. Cahn)
  (Foreword by Mary Ann Caws)
  Columbia University Press, 2013
*Happiness and Goodness: Philosophical Reflections on Living Well*
  (with Christine Vitrano)
  (Foreword by Robert B. Talisse)
  Columbia University Press, 2015
*Religion Within Reason*
  Columbia University Press, 2017
*Teaching Philosophy: A Guide*
  Routledge, 2018
*Inside Academia: Professors, Politics, and Policies*
  Rutgers University Press, 2019
*The Road Traveled and Other Essays*
  Wipf and Stock, 2019
*Philosophical Adventures*
  Broadview Press, 2019
*A Philosopher's Journey: Essays from Six Decades*
  Wipf and Stock, 2020
*Navigating Academic Life: How the System Works*
  Routledge, 2021

## Books Edited

*Philosophy of Art and Aesthetics: From Plato to Wittgenstein*
  (with Frank A. Tillman)
  Harper & Row, 1969
*The Philosophical Foundations of Education*
  Harper & Row, 1970
*Philosophy of Religion*
  Harper & Row, 1970
*Classics of Western Philosophy*
  Hackett Publishing Company, 1977
  Second Edition, 1985
  Third Edition, 1990
  Fourth Edition, 1995
  Fifth Edition, 1999
  Sixth Edition, 2003

Seventh Edition, 2007
Eighth Edition, 2012
*New Studies in the Philosophy of John Dewey*
  University Press of New England, 1977
*Scholars Who Teach: The Art of College Teaching*
  Nelson-Hall Company, 1978
  Wipf and Stock Publishers, 2004
*Contemporary Philosophy of Religion*
  (with David Shatz)
  Oxford University Press, 1982
*Reason at Work: Introductory Readings in Philosophy*
  (with Patricia Kitcher and George Sher)
  Harcourt Brace Jovanovich, 1984
  Second Edition, 1990
  Third Edition (also with Peter J. Markie), 1995
*Morality, Responsibility, and the University: Studies in Academic Ethics*
  Temple University Press, 1990
*Affirmative Action and the University: A Philosophical Inquiry*
  Temple University Press, 1993
*Twentieth-Century Ethical Theory*
  (with Joram G. Haber)
  Prentice Hall, 1995
*The Affirmative Action Debate*
  Routledge, 1995
  Second Edition, 2002
*Classics of Modern Political Theory: Machiavelli to Mill*
  Oxford University Press, 1997
*Classic and Contemporary Readings in the Philosophy of Education*
  McGraw Hill, 1997
  Second Edition, Oxford University Press, 2012
*Ethics: History, Theory, and Contemporary Issues*
  (with Peter Markie)
  Oxford University Press, 1998
  Second Edition, 2002
  Third Edition, 2006
  Fourth Edition, 2009
  Fifth Edition, 2012
  Sixth Edition, 2015
  Seventh Edition, 2020

*Exploring Philosophy: An Introductory Anthology*
   Oxford University Press, 2000
   Second Edition, 2005
   Third Edition, 2009
   Fourth Edition, 2012
   Fifth Edition, 2015
   Sixth Edition, 2018
   Seventh Edition, 2021
*Classics of Political and Moral Philosophy*
   Oxford University Press, 2002
   Second Edition, 2012
*Questions About God: Today's Philosophers Ponder the Divine*
   (with David Shatz)
   Oxford University Press, 2002
*Morality and Public Policy*
   (with Tziporah Kasachkoff)
   Prentice Hall, 2003
*Knowledge and Reality*
   (with Maureen Eckert and Robert Buckley)
   Prentice Hall, 2003
*Philosophy for the 21st Century: A Comprehensive Reader*
   Oxford University Press, 2003
*Ten Essential Texts in the Philosophy of Religion*
   Oxford University Press, 2005
*Political Philosophy: The Essential Texts*
   Oxford University Press, 2005
   Second Edition, 2011
   Third Edition, 2015
   Fourth Edition, 2021
*Philosophical Horizons: Introductory Readings*
   (with Maureen Eckert)
   Thomson/Wadsworth, 2006
   Second Edition, 2012
*Aesthetics: A Comprehensive Anthology*
   (with Aaron Meskin)
   Blackwell, 2008
   Second Edition (with Stephanie Ross and Sandra Shapshay), 2020
*Happiness: Classic and Contemporary Readings*
   (with Christine Vitrano)
   Oxford University Press, 2008

*The Meaning of Life, 3rd Edition: A Reader*
  (with E. M. Klemke)
  Oxford University Press, 2008
  Fourth Edition, 2018
*Seven Masterpieces of Philosophy*
  Pearson Longman, 2008
*The Elements of Philosophy: Readings from Past and Present*
  (with Tamar Szabó Gendler and Susanna Siegel)
  Oxford University Press, 2008
*Exploring Philosophy of Religion: An Introductory Anthology*
  Oxford University Press, 2009
  Second Edition, 2016
*Exploring Ethics: An Introductory Anthology*
  Oxford University Press, 2009
  Second Edition, 2011
  Third Edition, 2014
  Fourth Edition, 2017
  Fifth Edition, 2020
*Philosophy of Education: The Essential Texts*
  Routledge, 2009
*Political Problems*
  (with Robert B. Talisse)
  Prentice Hall, 2011
*Thinking About Logic: Classic Essays*
  (with Robert B. Talisse and Scott F. Aikin)
  Westview Press, 2011
*Fate, Time, and Language: An Essay on Free Will by David Foster Wallace*
  (with Maureen Eckert)
  Columbia University Press, 2011
*Moral Problems in Higher Education*
  Temple University Press, 2011
*Political Philosophy in the Twenty-First Century*
  (with Robert B. Talisse)
  Westview Press, 2013
*Portraits of American Philosophy*
  Rowman & Littlefield, 2013
*Reason and Religions: Philosophy Looks at the World's Religious Beliefs*
  Wadsworth/Cengage Learning, 2014

*Freedom and the Self: Essays on the Philosophy of David Foster Wallace*
  (with Maureen Eckert)
  Columbia University Press, 2015
*The World of Philosophy*
  Oxford University Press, 2016
  Second Edition, 2019
*Principles of Moral Philosophy: Classic and Contemporary Approaches*
  (with Andrew T. Forcehimes)
  Oxford University Press, 2017
*Foundations of Moral Philosophy: Readings in Metaethics*
  (with Andrew T. Forcehimes)
  Oxford University Press, 2017
*Exploring Moral Problems: An Introductory Anthology*
  (with Andrew T. Forcehimes)
  Oxford University Press, 2018
*Philosophers in the Classroom: Essays on Teaching*
  (with Alexandra Bradner and Andrew Mills)
  Hackett Publishing Company, 2018
The *Annotated Kant: Groundwork for the Metaphysics of Morals*
  Rowman & Littlefield, 2020

# About the Author

Steven M. Cahn is Professor Emeritus of Philosophy at the City University of New York Graduate Center, where he served for nearly a decade as Provost and Vice President for Academic Affairs, then as Acting President.

He was born in Springfield, Massachusetts, in 1942, and earned his A.B. from Columbia College in 1963 and his Ph.D. in philosophy from Columbia University in 1966. After having performed extensively as a pianist and organist, he embarked on a professorial career that included positions at Dartmouth College, Vassar College, New York University, the University of Rochester, and the University of Vermont, where he chaired the Department of Philosophy.

He served as a program officer at the Exxon Education Foundation, as Acting Director for Humanities at the Rockefeller Foundation, and as the first Director of General Programs at the National Endowment for the Humanities. He formerly chaired the American Philosophical Association's Committee on the Teaching of Philosophy, was the Association's Delegate to the American Council of Learned Societies, and was longtime President of the John Dewey Foundation, where he initiated the John Dewey Lectures, now delivered at every national meeting of the American Philosophical Association.

He is the author or editor of more than 60 books, and his numerous articles have appeared in a broad spectrum of publications, including *The Journal of Philosophy*, *The Chronicle of Higher Education*, *Shakespeare Quarterly*, *The American Journal of Medicine*, *The New Republic*, and *The New York Times*.

A collection of essays written in his honor, edited by two of his former doctoral students, Robert B. Talisse of Vanderbilt University and Maureen Eckert of the University of Massachusetts Dartmouth, is titled *A Teacher's Life: Essays for Steven M. Cahn* (Rowman & Littlefield, 2009; rpt. Wipf and Stock Publishers, 2021).

# Index

identity 9; impact on obtaining appointment 9–12, 94; specializations and job listings 11
diversity *see* affirmative action
Doney, Willis 113
Duggan, Timothy 113

ethics, link between manners 106–107
examinations *see* testing and teaching
Exxon Education Foundation 119

faculty appointments: advertising 78–79; assessing department's needs 75–80; departmental voting 91–92; impact of dissertation choice 9–12; interviewing candidates 93–96; search process 79–80
faculty reappointments 67
faculty search process 79–80; *see also* faculty appointments
Fox, Michael 65–66
Fox, Myron L. *see* Fox, Michael
Frankel, Charles 66–67
Frankfurt, Harry 24–25

Gendler, Tamar Szabó 34
Gert, Bernard 113
grade inflation 55–56
grading on a curve 54–55
grading system 51–57; as aid 51; basis for grade 53–54; ethics 56; fairness of grade 52–53; grade inflation 55–56; grading on a curve 54–55;

high grades, awarding 55; letters of evaluation 51–52; measure of level of achievement 52; misuse of 53–57; simple explanation of 53
graduate orientation 3–7; advice for doctoral students 4–7; approach to 3–4; message of 4; publishing opportunity 4; research area 4; teaching responsibilities 4
graduate school: dissertation topic, choosing 9–12; hidden curriculum 13–15; mistreatments/setbacks 24–25; orientation 3–7; preparing graduate students to teach 17–21; relationship building 24; reunions 23–25; sense of belonging to group 24

Hobbes, Thomas 106
Hook, Sidney 115, 116
humor, use of 18, 20
Humphries, Rolfe 109

interests, diversifying 6
interviews, faculty candidates 93–96; academic life question 95; best questions 94; dissertation topic 94; intellectual horizon 94–95; note taking 94; pace of questions 94; pedagogical questions 95; personal questions 95; polite attitude toward candidates 95; questions to ask 93; time limitations 94

job listings, specializations in demand 11

Kekes, John 84
Kitcher, Patricia 118
Kitcher, Philip 118

Mann, William 118
manners, link between ethics 106–107
motivation *see* students, motivating/engaging

Nagel, Ernest 109–110
National Endowment for the Humanities 119
networking 5
New York University: Educational Policy Committee 115–116; Washington Square College 115–117
Nozick, Robert 106

O'Connor, John 114
organization, key element of teaching 39–40

pedagogic techniques; *see also* teaching: basis of teacher evaluations 63; caring about students 29–31; elements of sound instruction for effective instruction 17–21; interviews with faculty candidates 95; pitfalls 60; sharing advice 71
*Philosophical Explanations* (Nozick) 106
preferential affirmative action *see* affirmative action

presentations: clarity in presentations 40–42; discussion opportunities 19; eye contact 20; pace of talk 19–20, 40; polished 19–20; stage fright 18; steps in reasoning 41–42; use of terminology 40–41
procedural affirmative action *see* affirmative action
promotion decisions 67
publishing opportunities 4, 5; key advancement 29–30

Quine, Willard Van Orman 42, 114

Rachels, James 116
Rawls, John 114
reading lists 4
reappointment decisions *see* faculty reappointments
reasoning, steps in 41–42
researcher/research productivity: focus on 21, 29; prestige as 13; subfields 75
Rockefeller Foundation 119

sexual harassment/abuse 6
Sher, George 118
speaking, pace of 19–20, 40
stereotyping 85; *see also* affirmative action
students; *see also* grading system; teaching; testing and teaching; appreciation extended to 106–107; caring about 29–31, 71; evaluating achievement 47; motivating/engaging 6, 18–20, 34–35,

37–38, 42; scope and depth of understanding 45; teacher ratings 63–68; teaching all students 33–35